MONITRESS MERLE

Angela Brazil

1st WORLD
LIBRARY
Literary Society

Monitress Merle

Angela Brazil

© 1st World Library, 2006
PO Box 2211
Fairfield, IA 52556
www.1stworldlibrary.com
First Edition

LCCN: 2006907699

Softcover ISBN: 1-4218-2417-5
Hardcover ISBN: 1-4218-2317-9
eBook ISBN: 1-4218-2517-1

Purchase *"Monitress Merle"*
as a traditional bound book at:
www.1stWorldLibrary.com/purchase.asp?ISBN=1-4218-2417-5

1st World Library is a literary, educational organization
dedicated to:

- Creating a free internet library of downloadable ebooks

- Hosting writing competitions and offering book
publishing scholarships.

Interested in more 1st World Library books?
contact: literacy@1stworldlibrary.com
Check us out at: www.1stworldlibrary.com

1st World Library Literary Society

Giving Back to the World

"If you want to work on the core problem, it's early school literacy."

- James Barksdale, former CEO of Netscape

"No skill is more crucial to the future of a child, or to a democratic and prosperous society, than literacy."

- Los Angeles Times

Literacy... means far more than learning how to read and write... The aim is to transmit... knowledge and promote social participation."

- UNESCO

"Literacy is not a luxury, it is a right and a responsibility. If our world is to meet the challenges of the twenty-first century we must harness the energy and creativity of all our citizens."

- President Bill Clinton

"Parents should be encouraged to read to their children, and teachers should be equipped with all available techniques for teaching literacy, so the varying needs and capacities of individual kids can be taken into account."

- Hugh Mackay

CONTENTS

CHAPTER I

A LAST BATHE

The warm, mellow September sunshine was streaming over the irregular roofs and twisted chimneys of the little town of Chagmouth, and was glinting on the water in the harbour, and sending gleaming, straggling, silver lines over the deep reflections of the shipping moored by the side of the jetty. The rising tide, lapping slowly and gently in from the ocean, was floating the boats beached on the shingle, and was gradually driving back the crowd of barefooted children who had ventured out in search of mussels, and was sending them, shrieking with mirth, scampering up the seaweed-covered steps that led to the fish market. On the crag-top above the town the corn had been cut, and harvesters were busy laying the sheaves together in stooks. The yellow fields shone in the afternoon light as if the hill were crowned with gold.

Walking along the narrow cobbled path that led past the harbour and up on to the cliff, Mavis and Merle looked at the scene around with that sense of rejoicing proprietorship with which we are wont to revisit the pet place of our adoption. It was two whole months since they had been in Chagmouth, and as they both considered the little town to be the absolute hub of the universe it was really a great event to find themselves once more in its familiar streets. They had spent the summer holidays with their father and mother in the north, and had come back to Durracombe just in time for the reopening of school. On this first Saturday after their return to

Devonshire they had motored with Uncle David to his branch surgery at Chagmouth, and were looking forward to several hours of amusement while he visited his patients at the sanatorium.

Readers who have followed the adventures of Mavis and Merle Ramsay in *A Fortunate Term* will remember that the sisters, on account of Mavis's health, had come to live with their great-uncle Dr. Tremayne at Durracombe, where they attended school daily at 'The Moorings.' Dr. Ramsay, their father, had decided shortly to leave his practice at Whinburn and go into partnership with Dr. Tremayne, but the removal to Devonshire could not take place till nearly Christmas, so the girls were to spend another term in sole charge of Uncle David, Aunt Nellie, and Jessop the elderly housekeeper, an arrangement which, though they were sorry to be parted from their parents, pleased them uncommonly well. It was a favourite excursion of theirs to accompany their uncle on Saturdays when he motored to visit patients at Chagmouth. On these occasions they would have lunch and tea with him at Grimbal's Farm, where he had his surgery, and would spend the intervening time on the seashore or wandering along the cliffs. To-day, tempted by the brilliant sunshine, they had brought their bathing costumes, towels, and tea-basket, and meant to secure the last dip of the holidays in case the weather should change and further mermaiding should prove impossible. They chatted briskly as they climbed the path up the cliff.

"Too bad Bevis has gone back to school! I thought we should just have seen him before he went!"

"And Tudor too! I met Babbie, while you were inside Carlyon's shop buying chocs, and she told me Tudor started yesterday, and Gwen went last Tuesday to a boarding-school near London. It was decided quite in a hurry because there happened to be a vacancy for her. It's a very fashionable school where they take the girls out to theatres and concerts and all sorts of places. Gwen's fearfully thrilled to go. They wanted to send her there before, only they couldn't get her in. Somebody else has left unexpectedly though, so there was a cubicle at liberty for her."

"It will just suit Gwen! But she'll miss her riding. She nearly lived on Taffy's back as a rule. Won't it be very lonely for Babbie all by herself with a governess? Will she come to school for French and dancing as usual?"

"She's coming to 'The Moorings' altogether. They're going to motor her over every day, and fetch her back at four. She's quite pleased about it. She always liked 'The Moorings' much better than Gwen did."

"And 'The Moorings,' from all reports, is going to be an utterly different school this term!"

"So I suppose! Hope it won't be too much changed, that's all! A new teacher, hot from a High School, means a new broom that will sweep very clean. It strikes me those nice do-as-you-please lessons with Miss Fanny will be dreams of the past, and we shall have to set our brains to work and swat! Ugh! It's not a particularly delirious prospect!"

Mavis laughed.

"Don't wrinkle your forehead into quite so many kinks! You look about forty!" she objected. "It mayn't turn out as hard as you expect. Anyhow, don't let us spoil the last Saturday of the holidays with thinking about it. I want to enjoy this afternoon thoroughly. I feel as if I'd been away from Chagmouth for years and years. Isn't it priceless to see it again? Have a chocolate! Or would you rather take a piece of toffee?"

The two girls had been mounting steadily as they talked, and were now walking along a narrow track which led along the top of the cliffs. Below them lay the gorgeous-hued crags of the rugged coast and a great expanse of sea, silver at the horizon, blue at mid-distance, and deep metallic green where it touched the shore. Innumerable sea-birds wheeled and screamed below, and the incoming tide lapped with little white waves over the reefs of rocks, and submerged the pools where gobies were darting about, and sea-anemones were stretching out crimson or green tentacles, and scurrying crabs were hiding among masses of brown oar-weed. Above and beyond was a network of brambles, where ripe blackberries hung in such tempting clusters that it was hardly in human nature to resist them, and Merle, with purple-stained fingers, loitered and lingered to enjoy the feast.

"If you're not quick the tide will have turned and it won't be half so nice to bathe!" urged Mavis impatiently. "Do hurry up now, and you can absolutely gorge on blackberries as we come back, if you want to. I'll promise to wait for you then."

"Right-o! I'm coming! Though I must just get that one big beauty! There! I won't eat a single one more till I've had my dip. We must be close to the cove now. I'll run if you like!"

The bathing-place for which the girls were bound was a sandy creek among the rocks. A hundred years ago it had been a favourite spot for smugglers to land contraband goods, and a series of steps cut in the cliff testified to its former use. Nowadays it was commonly deserted, and in the early part of the summer, when Mavis and Merle had been wont to visit it, they had had it all to themselves. They had gone there so often and found it untenanted that they had come to regard it as their private property, and, in consequence, they were most unreasonably annoyed, when climbing down the steps, to hear sounds of laughter rising up from below.

"Who's in *our* cove?" demanded Merle sharply, somewhat as Father Bruin asked the immortal question, "Who's sleeping on *my* bed?"

"All the world, I should say!" replied the aggrieved voice of Mavis, who was in front and had first view of the scene beneath. "The place is an absolute 'seaside resort.' Never saw so many people in my life before! Where do they all come from?"

The little cove, *their* cove, which in June had been so delightfully secluded and retired, was undoubtedly invaded by quite a number of visitors. Children were paddling or scampering along the sands, wet heads were bobbing in and out of the water, every rocky crevice was in use as a dressing-room, picnic parties were taking tea on the rocks, and a circle of boys and girls were playing a noisy game at the brink of the waves. Very ruefully Mavis and Merle descended to swell the throng. It was not at all the sort of bathe which they had anticipated, and, had there been another available spot within reach, they would have utterly disdained it.

"Shall we go on to Yellow Head?" ventured Merle hesitatingly.

"There isn't time. The tide would be out before we got there, and it's a perfect tangle of oar-weed unless the water's high. Never mind! There'll be elbow-room in the sea at any rate. There's a corner here where we can undress. Come along! O-o-h! There's some one else inside!"

"We're just ready! You can come in if you like!" proclaimed a voice, as two girls in navy bathing costumes and rubber caps issued from behind a rock, and running swiftly down the sand plunged into the water.

Availing themselves of the opportunity Mavis and Merle took temporary possession of the naiads' dressing-room, and in the course of a few minutes more were revelling in a swim. The red rubber caps of the girls who preceded them were plainly to be seen some distance from the shore, where their owners were apparently having a race towards a rock that jutted from the waves.

"Oh, they *mustn't* go out there! There's an awful current! Bevis warned us about it!" gasped Mavis, swimming securely with one foot on the ground. "Can't we stop them?

Shout, Merle!"

"Hello, there! Ahoy! Come back!" yelled Merle, who possessed stronger lungs than her sister. "They don't hear me! Coo-oo-ee! That's done it, thank goodness! Come - back - you're - going - to - get - into - a - current!"

The two red caps, warned in time of their danger, turned and swam into safer waters. They did not venture so far again from the shore, but frolicked with some companions, trying to make wheels and to perform various other feats of agility, which were generally failures and ended in a splash. They were so long about it that Mavis and Merle went from the water first and had time to dress quite leisurely before the others, shaking out wet fair hair, followed to the crevice among the rocks.

The Ramsays took their picnic basket, and, climbing a short way up the steps, settled themselves upon a grassy platform which afforded a good view of the cove below. They liked this vantage-ground better than the sands, and began to spread out the cups and saucers and parcels of cakes which Jessop had packed for them, congratulating themselves upon having a spot at least fairly apart. But they were not destined to spend that afternoon in solitary state. They had scarcely opened their basket when three heads came bobbing up the steps, shamelessly invaded their platform, and also began to unpack tea-cups.

Merle, who did not like other people to trespass upon her rights, frowned and turned her back upon them, and probably each little party would have taken its meal separately had not an unforeseen and utterly untoward accident happened. Mavis knocked their thermos flask with her elbow and sent it spinning over the cliff. Here was a pretty business! Their tea was gone, and the flask, if they found it, would be utterly smashed.

"It's not worth climbing down to pick it up!" lamented Mavis contritely. "I'm so sorry, Merle! It was horribly clumsy of me!"

Angela Brazil

"Do have some of ours!" suggested one of the strangers sympathetically. "We've heaps! Two flasks; and that's more than we shall drink ourselves. You might just as well!"

"I say, it was awfully decent of you to call to us not to go on to those rocks!" put in another. "We didn't know about the current."

The third girl made no remark, but she smiled invitingly and held out one of their flasks.

So it came about that Mavis and Merle moved nearer and joined the others, so that they formed one party. For a few minutes they sat in polite silence, taking in the items of their neighbours' appearance. When the Ramsays compared notes afterwards they decided that they had never before seen three such pretty girls. The two who had worn the red bathing caps were evidently sisters, for they had the same clear-cut features, fair complexions, cupid mouths, and beautiful dark-fringed eyes. Their companion, whose brown hair was drying in the breeze, was a complete contrast, with her warm brunette colouring and quick vivacious manner, "like an orchid between two roses," as Mavis described her later. It was she who spoke first - quite a conventional inquiry but decidedly to the point.

"Are you staying in Chagmouth?" she asked.

"We've only come over for the day from Durracombe," answered Merle.

The three strangers looked immediately interested.

"Durracombe! Why, we're going to start school there next week!"

"Never at 'The Moorings'!" gasped Merle excitedly.

"That's the place! Do you go there too? Oh! I say! Do tell us all about it! We've been just crazy to know what it's like. You two look sports! What are your names? Are the rest of the school jolly, and is Miss Pollard nice?"

With such a common interest as 'The Moorings' to talk about, the ice was completely broken, and the five girls were soon chatting in friendly fashion.

Mavis and Merle, having given a few details about themselves and how they often motored over to Chagmouth with Dr. Tremayne, drew in turn some information from their new acquaintants. The two fair-haired girls, aged respectively fourteen and thirteen, were Beata and Romola Castleton, and their father, an artist, had lately removed from Porthkeverne in Cornwall, and had taken a house at Chagmouth. Their friend Fay Macleod, a year older than Beata, was an American, whose father had come to Europe in search of health, and being attracted to Chagmouth by his love of sketching, had settled there temporarily for a rest-cure, and was enjoying the quiet and beauty of the quaint place and its surrounding scenery.

"I suppose you'll all be weekly boarders?" ventured Mavis, when Fay had finished her communications.

"No, we're to be day-girls. Six of us from Chagmouth are joining in a car and motoring every morning and being fetched back at four - ourselves, Nan and Lizzie Colville, and Tattie Carew. It will be rather a squash to cram six of us into Vicary's car! We've named it 'the sardine-tin' already. I hope nobody else will want to join us!"

"Babbie Williams is to be a day-girl this term. She lives over there at The Warren."

"We haven't room for her."

"She's going in their own car."

"That's good news for the sardines! I was thinking some of us would have to ride on the footboard or the luggage-carrier. Is

Babbie fair, with bobbed hair? Then I've seen her in church. Seven of us from Chagmouth! We ought to make quite a clique in the school!"

"Oh, we don't want any cliques," said Merle quickly. "We had enough of that sort of thing when Opal was there. Miss Pollard told mother that the new mistress, Miss Mitchell, is going to reorganise everything, and bring it up to date, so I expect we shall find a great many changes when we start again. Have you been at school before?"

"Romola and I went to The Gables at Porthkeverne," replied Beata. "We loved it, and we were dreadfully sorry to leave. Fay, of course, has been at school in America."

"And we used to go to a big High school in the north until we came to Durracombe. 'The Moorings' seemed a tiny place at first, and then we grew to love it. We adore Miss Pollard and Miss Fanny. I hope you'll like them too! I'm so glad we've met you, because we'll know you when you arrive at school, and we can show you round. I'm afraid we shall have to be going now, because Uncle David will be back from the sanatorium and waiting for us. Thanks most immensely for the tea. We'll look out for you on Tuesday. Good-bye!"

As Mavis and Merle walked back along the cliffs to Chagmouth their tongues wagged fast in discussion of their new acquaintances. Mavis was charmed with Beata and Romola, and Merle had utterly lost her heart to Fay.

"I feel as if I could like her!" she declared. "She's a sport, and really we want somebody to wake us up a little at 'The Moorings.' I believe this term is going to be jolly. My spirits are rising and I see fun ahead. I only wish Daddy could go and live at Chagmouth and *we* could go to school every day in 'the sardine-tin.' They'll have the time of their lives, the luckers! Don't I envy them, just!"

"I don't think I'd like to be packed quite so tight, thanks!"

objected Mavis. "On the whole, I much prefer going backwards and forwards to Chagmouth in Uncle David's car. Merle! Do you know it's after five! We must simply scoot - oh, I daresay I did promise you might eat blackberries, but you haven't time now. You shouldn't have stayed so long at the cove if you wanted a blackberry feed! If you don't hurry up I shall run off and leave you and go home with Uncle David by myself! There! Oh, you're coming! Good! I thought you'd hardly care to spend the night upon the cliffs with the sea-gulls!"

CHAPTER II

A SCHOOL BALLOT

Mavis and Merle started for school on Tuesday morning confident of finding many changes. Hitherto 'The Moorings' had been a modest establishment where about twenty-four children had been educated by Miss Pollard and her sister Miss Fanny, who were the daughters of the late Vicar of the parish. They were neither of them particularly learned or up to date, but they had a happy knack with girls, and had been especially successful in the care of delicate pupils. The remarkably mild climate of Durracombe made the place peculiarly suitable for those who had been born in India or other hot countries, and so many more boarders had been entered for this term that the school was practically doubled. Recognising the fact that this sudden enlargement in numbers ought also to mean a march forward in other ways, the sisters were wise enough to seize their golden opportunity and completely reorganise their methods. They were fortunate in being able to get hold of the house next to their own, and, turning that into a hostel for boarders, they devoted the whole of 'The Moorings' to classrooms. They engaged a thoroughly competent and reliable mistress, with a university degree and High School experience, and gave her *carte blanche* to revise the curriculum and institute what innovations she thought fit. They allowed her to choose her own assistant mistress, and made fresh arrangements for visiting teachers, reserving for themselves only a very few of the classes, and concentrating most of their energies on the management of the hostel. These new plans gave great satisfaction to both parents and pupils.

"It will be rather nice to have somebody modern at the head of things, so long as Miss Pollard and Miss Fanny aren't entirely shelved," declared Merle.

"They're perfect dears! We couldn't do without them," agreed Mavis.

"But they're not clever!"

"Um - I don't know! It depends what you call clever! They mayn't be B.A.'s and all the rest of it, but they're well read, and they can sketch and sing and play and do a hundred things that a great many graduates can't. I call them 'cultured,' that's the right name for them. They're such absolute and perfect ladies. It's a style you really don't meet every day. And they're so pretty with their pink cheeks and their silver hair, like the sweet old-fashioned pictures of eighteenth-century beauties in powder and patches. I love to look at them, and to listen to the gentle refined way they talk - I think they're adorable!"

"So they are - but you want something more in a school. I hope the fresh teacher will be a regular sport, and that she'll use slang sometimes, and play hockey. That's my ideal of a head mistress."

Miss Mitchell, the new peg upon which so much was now to depend at 'The Moorings,' might not have been blamed for regarding Tuesday morning as somewhat of an ordeal. If she was nervous, however, she managed to conceal her feelings, and bore the introduction to her prospective pupils with cheerful calm.

Forty-six girls, taking mental stock of her, decided instantly that she was 'the right sort.' She was tall, in her middle twenties, had a fresh complexion, light brown hair, a brisk decisive manner, and a pleasant twinkle in her hazel eyes. She was evidently not in the least afraid of her audience, a fact which at once gave her the right handle. She faced their united stare smilingly.

"I'm very pleased to meet you all!" she began. "I hope we shall work together splendidly and have an extremely happy term. As Miss Pollard has just told you, there have been so many changes at 'The Moorings' that it is practically a new school. It's a tremendous opportunity to be able to make a fresh start like this. We can make our own traditions and our own rules. Some of you have been at the school before and some have been at other schools, but I want you all to forget past traditions and unite together to make 'The Moorings' the biggest success that can possibly be. We're all going to love it and to be very loyal to it. We hope to do well with our work, and well with our games. I must explain to you later about all the various societies which we mean to start, but I want to tell you that though there is plenty of work in front of you there's also plenty of fun, and that if every girl makes up her mind to do her very best all round we shall get on grandly. Now I am going to read out the lists of the various forms, and then you can march away in turn to your own classrooms."

In making her arrangements for the reorganisation of the school Miss Mitchell had decided to have no Sixth form as yet. The girls were all under seventeen, and she did not consider any of them sufficiently advanced to be placed in so high a position. The Fifth was at present to be the top form, and consisted of eleven girls, all of whom she intended should work their uttermost and fit themselves for the honour of becoming the Sixth a year later.

Mavis and Merle, both of whom were included in this elect eleven, walked demurely away to their new classroom. Five of their old companions were with them, Iva Westwood, Nesta Pitman, Aubrey Simpson, Muriel Burnitt, and Edith Carey, and the remaining four consisted of Beata Castleton, Fay Macleod, and two strangers, Sybil Vernon and Kitty Trefyre. Romola Castleton had been placed in the Fourth, together with Maude Carey, Babbie Williams, Nan Colville, Tattie

Carew, and several other new girls.

The Fifth, as the top form, was to be mainly Miss Mitchell's; Miss Barnes, the fresh assistant mistress, was to take the Fourth; and the teaching of the three lower forms would be shared by Miss Hopkins, Mademoiselle, and Miss Fanny Pollard. Lessons, on a first morning, are usually more or less haphazard, but at any rate a beginning was made, the pupils were entered on their class registers, their capacities were tested, and they began in some slight degree to know their teachers. Before the school separated at 12.30 for dinner Miss Pollard had an announcement to make.

"Miss Mitchell and I have decided that for the general good of the school it will be wise to appoint four monitresses. Two of these must be boarders and will be chosen by us, but the other two may be elected by yourselves. We will have a ballot this afternoon. You may nominate any girls you like by writing their names upon slips of paper and handing them in to me before 2.30. All candidates, however, must be over the age of fifteen and must have spent at least two previous terms at 'The Moorings.' The voting will take place in the big schoolroom immediately after four o'clock."

Mavis and Merle, walking home to lunch at Bridge House, discussed the project eagerly as they went.

"Good for Miss Pollard! Or I expect it's really Miss Mitchell who suggested it! I call it a ripping idea. It's just exactly what's wanted. The monitresses will lead the games and all the various societies. Run the school, in fact. What sport!" rejoiced Merle, with shining eyes. "The old 'Moorings' will really wake up at last."

"Only four monitresses, and two of them are to be boarders and chosen by the powers that be!" mused Mavis. "That means Iva and Nesta, if I know anything of Miss Pollard and Miss Fanny! Now the question is who are to be the other two lucky ones?"

"It ought to be somebody who could lead!" flushed Merle. "Somebody really good at games and able to organise all that rabble of kids. Some one who's been accustomed to a big school and knows what ought to be done. Not girls who've spent all their lives in a tiny school like this. They've no standards. I've often told them that! They've simply no idea of how things used to swing at the Whinburn High!"

"I wish Miss Pollard and Miss Mitchell would have done all the choosing," said Mavis anxiously. "I think myself it's a mistake to put it to the vote. Probably somebody quite unsuitable will be elected. The juniors will plump for the girl they like best, without caring whether she knows anything about games or not. There's Aubrey Simpson!"

"Oh! They *can't* choose 'the jackdaw'!" interrupted Merle.

"They can choose her if they like. She's over fifteen and perfectly eligible. Edith Carey is rather a favourite, I believe."

"That silly goose! Good-night!"

"Well, there's Muriel Burnitt at any rate. She's been a long time at 'The Moorings.'"

"All the worse for that, though she's better than Edith or Aubrey. I shall vote for her myself, and for you."

"And I'm going to vote for *you*, and for Muriel, because, as you say, she's better than the others. I sincerely hope you'll win."

"I hope we both shall. I'll nominate you if you'll nominate me!"

"Rather a family affair, isn't it? I think I'll ask first and see if anybody else is going to give in our names. Perhaps Iva or Nesta may. It would be much nicer than seeming to poke ourselves forward."

"If we don't hustle a little we'll never get there! That's my opinion! You're too good for this wicked world, Mavis! I've often told you so!" declared Merle, running into the house and putting down her books with a slam. "Angel girls are all very well at home, but school is a scrimmage and it's those who fight who come up on top! Don't laugh! Oh, I enjoy fighting! I tell you I want most desperately and tremendously to be made a monitress, and if I'm not chosen, well - it will be the disappointment of my life! I'm not joking! I mean it really and truly. I've set my heart upon it."

Mavis, who had a very fine sense of the fitness of things, and who did not think sisters should nominate one another, returned early to school that afternoon and hunted up Iva Westwood. She found her very enthusiastic about the election.

"We've never had anything of the sort before at 'The Moorings,'" purred Iva. "We're beginning to wake up here, aren't we? I'm going to give in your name as a candidate, Mavis! I'm just writing it now."

"Thanks! Won't you put Merle too?"

"Oh, I will if you like." (Iva's voice was not too enthusiastic.) "I suppose it doesn't matter how many we nominate. Somehow I never thought of Merle."

"She's a splendid leader, and A1 at games. You should have seen her at Whinburn High!"

"Oh, I daresay! Well, to please you I'll put her name on my list. It can do no harm at any rate."

"Thanks ever so!"

"Old Muriel's canvassing like anything downstairs among the kids!"

"Is canvassing allowed?"

"Well, it hasn't been forbidden. Nesta and I are too proud to go and beg for votes, but Mu doesn't care in the least; rather enjoys it, in fact. She's sitting in the playroom, with Florrie Leach and Betty Marshall on her knee, 'doing the popular,' and giving away whole packets of sweets. If Merle really wants - hello! here's Merle herself!"

Mavis turned quickly, for her younger sister, looking flushed and excited, had burst suddenly into the room and was speaking eagerly.

"Mavis! Have you a shilling in your pocket? I left my purse at home! *Do* lend it to me! What for? I want to tear out and buy some sweets. Oh yes, I've time. I shall simply sprint. Hand it over, that's a saintly girl! Thanks immensely!"

Merle departed like a whirlwind, slamming the door after her. Iva Westwood pulled an expressive grimace and laughed.

"So she's trying the popular trick too! Well, sometimes it works and sometimes it doesn't. I think Edith Carey has a good chance myself. The kids are rather fond of her. Have you written your nominations yet, Mavis? Then come along, and we'll drop them inside the box."

As the first bell rang at 2.25 and the girls began to assemble in the big schoolroom, Muriel Burnitt walked in followed by a perfect comet's tail of juniors, some of whom were hanging on to her arms. Each was sucking a peppermint bull's-eye, and each wore a piece of pink ribbon pinned on to her dress.

"Muriel's favours!" they explained, giggling loudly. "We're all of us going to vote for her. Isn't it fun?"

Mavis glanced round for Merle, hoping her expedition to the sweet-shop would not have made her late, and to her relief saw her sitting on the opposite side of the room, in company with Beata and Romola Castleton, Fay Macleod, and a number of other new girls whose acquaintance she had evidently just made. They were passing round chocolates, and seemingly enjoying themselves. Merle waved a hand gaily at her sister, beckoning her to join the group, but at that moment Miss Mitchell entered the room, and all seated themselves on the nearest available benches while the roll-call was taken.

"We will meet here at four o'clock for the election," said the mistress, as she closed the register and dismissed the various forms to their classrooms.

The first day of a new term always seems intolerably long, and with such an interesting event as a ballot before them most of the girls felt the hour and a half to drag, and turned many surreptitious glances towards wrist watches. Merle in especial, who hated French translation, groaned as she looked up words in the dictionary, and made several stupid mistakes, because her thoughts were focussed on the election instead of on the matter in hand. Once she yawned openly, and drew down a reproof from Mademoiselle, whereupon she heaved a submissive sigh, controlled her boredom, and went on wearily transferring the flowery sentiments of Fenelon into the English tongue. At precisely five minutes to four the big bell clanged out a warning, dictionaries were shut, exercise-books handed in, pencil-boxes replaced in desks, and the class filed downstairs to the big schoolroom. Miss Pollard was not there: she was busy in the hostel; and Miss Fanny, looking rather flustered and nervous, had evidently given over the conduct of the meeting to Miss Mitchell, and was present merely as a spectator. The new mistress seemed perfectly at home and ready for the occasion. She passed round pieces of paper, inquired whether everybody had a pencil, then made her announcements.

"As Miss Pollard told you this morning, you are here to elect two monitresses. Two from among the boarders have already been chosen by us, these are Iva Westwood and Nesta Pitman, but the remaining two are to be balloted for from among the list of candidates. As perhaps some of you don't understand a ballot, I will tell you just what to do. I have written on the blackboard the names of those girls who have been nominated:

"Muriel Burnitt.

"Aubrey Simpson.

"Edith Carey.

"Mavis Ramsay.

"Merle Ramsay.

"What I want you to do is to write on your piece of paper the names of the two candidates for whom you wish to vote, then fold your paper and hand it in. You must not add your own name to it, and you have no need to tell anybody how you voted. The whole principle of a ballot is that it is done in secret. Are you ready? Then please begin."

The little ceremony was soon over, the girls scribbled rapidly, folded their papers, and passed them along the benches to Nesta and Iva, who collected them and gave them to Miss Mitchell.

"It will take a short time to count the votes," explained the mistress. "Those girls who wish to go home can do so, but any who like to wait and hear the result can stay."

Miss Mitchell and Miss Fanny retired to the study and the meeting broke up. Most of the day-girls put on their hats and coats in readiness to go home, but hung about the hall until the names should be announced. The contingent from Chagmouth, whose car was stationed outside in the road, and whose driver was waxing impatient, were obliged to depart without the exciting news. Merle went as far as the gate to watch them pack into their 'sardine-tin.' Four sat behind, and two in front with the chauffeur, all quite radiant and thoroughly enjoying themselves.

"Good-bye! I hope you'll win!" said Beata, waving a hand to Merle with difficulty, for she was tightly sandwiched between Fay and Tattie. "We did our best for you and Mavis. I didn't know any of those others. Romola, have you got the books? That's all right. I was afraid we'd left the satchel. Yes," (to the chauffeur) "we're quite ready now, thanks! Ta-ta, Merle! Good luck to you! We're off!"

Merle, looking after the retreating car, was joined by Aubrey Simpson, rather injured, and disconsolate.

"I didn't know all these new girls were to have votes," she grumbled. "How can *they* choose a monitress when they don't know anybody! It's rather humbug, isn't it?"

"They know *me*" perked Merle.

"Did you canvass them? Oh, how mean!"

"Why mean? You could have done it yourself. Muriel was canvassing among the juniors as hard as she could go."

"I might have canvassed among the new boarders! Why didn't I think of it?" wailed Aubrey.

"Well, really, it's your own stupid fault! Don't blame me!" snapped Merle.

"Iva and Nesta said they didn't mean to ask for votes."

"Well, they'd no need to. They were both jolly certain that Miss Pollard would make them monitresses. It's easy to talk loftily when you're sure of your innings."

"Did Mavis canvass?"

"No - but then, of course, Mavis wouldn't!"

"Why not?"

Angela Brazil

"Oh - because she's Mavis! I can't see her doing it somehow. What a long time Miss Mitchell and Miss Fanny are over their counting! I wish they'd hurry up. I want to go home to tea."

The girls had not much longer, however, to wait.

In the course of a few minutes the new mistress entered the hall and read out the important result.

"The polling is as follows," she announced.

"Muriel Burnitt............ 27
Mavis Ramsay 20
Merle Ramsay 19
Edith Carey.................. 14
Aubrey Simpson........... 12

"The two monitresses elected, therefore, are Muriel Burnitt and Mavis Ramsay."

Some of the girls raised a cheer, others took no notice; Miss Mitchell, who seemed in a hurry, vanished back into the study. The boarders, hearing their tea-bell, made for the hostel.

"Congrats, Mavis!" said Iva, as she walked away arm-in-arm with Nesta. "I'm glad the lot has fallen on you. Muriel was pretty sure of a walk-over, but it was a toss-up who was to be the fourth. I don't mind telling you I voted for you myself. And so did Nesta, I'm sure."

"It was a ballot, and I'm not going to let out whom I voted for!" declared Nesta. "Some people can't keep their own secrets! All the same, I'm glad it's you, Mavis. I wouldn't have had Aubrey a monitress for worlds."

The Ramsays walked home together along the High Street to Bridge House. Muriel Burnitt, escorted by Florrie and Viola Leach and the three little Andrews, was on in front, pluming herself upon her victory. The Careys had disappeared down the short cut to the Vicarage. Mavis hardly dared to look at Merle. The latter kept her face turned away and blinked her eyes hard. She had enough self-restraint not to weep openly in the High Street. When they reached their own door however, she bolted through the surgery entrance and, running into the garden, hid herself in the summer-house, whither Mavis, after a word to Aunt Nellie, presently followed her to offer what consolation she could.

"It's not that I'm jealous of *you*!" sobbed Merle stormily. "I wanted us both to win! What does Muriel know about a decent game of hockey, or how to conduct a society, or run a school magazine? It's idiotic that she should be chosen. Neither she nor Iva nor Nesta has ever been at a big school. A precious bungle they'll make of their meetings. I know *you'll* be there - but you're so gentle you'll never stand up against them, and they'll have everything their own silly way. 'The Moorings' won't be very much changed if it's just to be run upon the same old lines. I shan't bother to try and help. I might have done so much if they'd elected me, but what's the use now? I'm frightfully and frantically disappointed. If Miss Mitchell had had any sense she'd have waited a fortnight till she got to know the girls, and then have chosen the monitresses herself. If it's Miss Fanny's fault, I'm not friends with her any more! Tea-time, did you say? I suppose I shall have to come in then, though I really don't want any. Ugh! I hate everything!"

Tea that day was a dreary affair. Uncle David was out, Aunt Nellie had a headache so was unusually quiet, and Merle, with red eyes, sat silent and brooding. Mavis tried desperately to make a little conversation, but it was impossible to maintain a monologue, and she soon dropped the futile attempt. Merle, after eating half a piece of bread and butter and declining a chocolate biscuit, begged suddenly to be excused, and with two big unruly tears splashing down her cheeks fled from the room.

"Poor child! I'm afraid she's terribly disappointed," commented Aunt Nellie sympathetically.

"It seems a pity she wasn't chosen. I suppose she would have made a splendid monitress. It's half the battle to be keen about anything."

Mavis agreed, passed the cake, finished her tea, picked up the dropped stitches in Aunt Nellie's piece of knitting, carried a message to the cook, then went out into the garden. She wanted to be alone for a little while. There was a retired corner among the bushes by the wall overlooking the river. She had placed a box here for a seat, and called it her hermitage. Even Merle had not so far discovered it. It was a retreat where she could withdraw from everybody, and be absolutely uninterrupted and by herself. There was something about which she wished to think in quiet. The idea had been pressing upon her, clamouring in her brain ever since Miss Mitchell's announcement, but she must consider it carefully before she acted upon it. Sitting in her green nook, watching the golden light sparkling upon the river below, she faced her problem:

"Merle would really make a far better monitress than I should. Oughtn't I to give the post up to her?"

It was a struggle, and a very difficult one, for Mavis, quiet though she was, had her ambitions, and it would be hard to yield place to her younger sister. It is only those who are accustomed to practise self-control who have the strength for an emergency. She longed for the opportunity of helping the school, and to stand aside voluntarily and give the work up to another seemed a big sacrifice.

"It's got to be, though!" sighed Mavis. "I'll go down and see Miss Fanny about it at once. I expect I can make her understand."

Dodging Merle, who was disconsolately doing some gardening, she walked back to 'The Moorings' and went to the hostel. Miss Fanny, busy among the new boarders, received her with astonishment.

"What is it, Mavis? I can only spare you five minutes. You want to speak to me about the monitress-ship? My dear child, Miss Mitchell will explain everything to you to-morrow, and tell you exactly what you have to do. There's no need to trouble about it now."

"It isn't that, please, Miss Fanny!" blushed Mavis. "The fact of the matter is that I think Merle ought to have been chosen instead of me. I was only one mark ahead of her. She'd make a far better monitress than I should. May I resign and let her have the post instead?"

This was coming to the point with a vengeance. Miss Fanny knitted her eyebrows and pursed up her mouth into a button.

"I rather expected Merle to be elected," she admitted cautiously.

"She'd be splendid!" urged Mavis, pursuing her advantage. "She's a born leader. She's able to organise things and to keep order, and she's good at games. She'd throw herself heart and soul into it, and work tremendously at all the new schemes. She'd start clubs among the juniors as well as the seniors, and coach them in hockey, and do her level best! I'll guarantee she would!"

"And what about yourself? Can't you do any of these things?" questioned Miss Fanny.

"Not so well as Merle! I'm shyer, and I daren't speak out, and I'm not much good at games. And oh! Miss Fanny, there's another side of the question. I know Merle so well. If she's made monitress she'll be heart and soul for the school and an enormous help, but - she's a queer girl, and if she has no special place here or anything to concentrate her energy on, she may give trouble."

"That is certainly no reason for placing her in a post of authority," frowned Miss Fanny.

"No - but she's a girl who's always for or against, and it's so very important she should be on the right side. I believe this would be the making of her. She'd try for the sake of others when she wouldn't make any effort for herself."

"I believe you're right," conceded Miss Fanny thoughtfully. "Miss Mitchell would certainly be most relieved to have a monitress who was capable of organising the juniors at games. She was wondering how she was going to manage. Do I understand, then, that you wish to resign in favour of Merle?"

"Please! I'll help her all I can in the background."

"Very well, Mavis. I'll accept your resignation and announce the matter in school to-morrow. Now I must go, for I have a hundred things to do. Tell Merle to come five minutes earlier in the morning and I'll talk to her in the study. On the whole, I think the arrangement will be all for the best."

It was a very radiant, triumphant Mavis who ran home to the old garden, found Merle among the flowerbeds, and told her the glorious news.

"Sis! You can't mean it! Is it true? Oh, I don't like to take it! It's too good of you! Don't you really mind? It's all the world to *me*. I've been hoping to be made monitress ever since Miss Pollard spoke about reorganising the school. Won't I have the time of my life! Monitress Merle! It sounds nice, doesn't it? I must go and tell Jessop and Aunt Nellie! How astonished everybody will be in school to-morrow. Fay and Beata will be pleased. They were tremendously keen on my winning the ballot. I'm so glad about it I want to turn a somersault or do something mad. Come and dance with me, you old darling! What a trump you are! You're *sure* you don't mind?"

"Not a bit," said Mavis, swallowing a little lump in her throat. "Of course I'll be ready to help you with anything whenever you want me. There'll be plenty of hard work just at first, no doubt. You'll soon be up to your eyes in starting clubs and societies. Keep a corner for me on the school magazine if you found one. That's all I bargain for. I always liked the Literary Society at Whinburn High. My hearty congratulations to you, and every good wish for the success of everything you undertake - Miss Monitress Merle!"

CHAPTER III

THE NEW MONITRESS

The announcement of Mavis's resignation and the consequent promotion of Merle to the post of monitress was received at school with varying degrees of surprise. Some of the girls regretted it, others thought that in the circumstances it was a wise decision.

"On the whole, I'm glad," admitted Iva in private to Nesta. "I love Mavis, but she's too fine stuff for the job. It's like trying to cut sacking with your most delicate pair of scissors. Now Merle will slash away and won't mind anything. She's not afraid of those juniors, and really some of them need a tight hand, the young wretches. It would half kill Mavis to have to battle with them. Merle enjoys fighting."

"She'll get it, then," laughed Nesta. "There'll be plenty of scope for it in the school, and I daresay I shall have a scrimmage or two with her myself. Certainly Muriel will! Don't look shocked. We'll do our squabbles in private if we have any. To the rest of the world, of course, the four monitresses will seem absolutely at one about everything. We won't give ourselves away!"

In a school where hitherto there has been no strict standard of discipline, and which has suddenly doubled its numbers, it is rather a difficult matter to decide the absolute limits of authority. Miss Mitchell, new herself, gave the monitresses some general rules and directions but left them to make what she called 'their own by-laws.'

"Work as much as you can through committees, and have an occasional general meeting to voice popular opinion," she counselled. "Always keep your position as leaders, but don't degenerate into an oligarchy. Listen to just grievances, and try and bring everybody into harmony. The tone of the school will depend very largely upon you four. Remember it's a responsibility as well as an honour to have such a post of trust."

By the wish of both Miss Pollard and Miss Mitchell, it was arranged that Iva and Nesta, who were boarders, should busy themselves mostly with the affairs of the hostel, and that Muriel and Merle should look after those things which specially concerned the day-girls. There were, of course, various societies in which they could all unite, but the interests of both were to be equally balanced. In order that the girls should have time to inaugurate the numerous projects that loomed on the horizon, the last hour of the coming Thursday afternoon was set apart for the purpose, and a general meeting was to be held in the schoolroom.

"I shall leave you to manage it entirely yourselves," said Miss Mitchell. "Found your own clubs, make your own arrangements, and elect your own committees and officers. You can come and tell me about it afterwards."

Merle, rejoicing over the liberty thus given, found Iva, Nesta, and Muriel a trifle nervous and diffident.

"The fact of the matter is," admitted Iva ruefully, "we none of us know how to conduct a public meeting. What do you *do*? I've a vague idea that there ought to be a chairman and a secretary, but what else? Rather weak of us, isn't it? It seems so humiliating to go and tell Miss Mitchell we can't carry on! She'll think us queer monitresses. Merle, can you give any light?"

"We used to have heaps of public meetings at Whinburn High, and I think I know the ropes. I can coach you all up beforehand. I should say we'd better find out what girls are most likely to be of help, and arrange for them to be proposed as members of committees. There's Mavis, of course. Beata and Romola Castleton have been at school before, and so has Fay Macleod. Kitty Trefyre looks as if she might be useful."

"I shall propose that you take the chair," said Iva. "Oughtn't that to be a question of age?" interrupted Muriel quickly.

"It's a question of who is competent to do it. Merle's the only one of us who knows how," returned Nesta, looking Muriel squarely in the face.

"Oh, all right!" (rather sulkily).

"We shall want a secretary, and you're a quick writer," suggested Merle, with more tact than she generally possessed.

It was evident to Merle from the first that the greatest factor of trouble in connection with her new post would lie with Muriel Burnitt. Muriel was a little older than herself, she was clever, and she had a sharp tongue. She had been educated solely at 'The Moorings,' and she very much resented any allusions by Merle to former doings at the Whinburn High school. Iva and Nesta were more broad-minded, and were quite ready to take the benefit of Merle's past experiences, but as their work lay largely at the hostel they were not so likely to clash. Even Muriel, however, recognised the necessity of receiving instruction on the subject of a public meeting, and allowed herself to be duly coached for the duties of the occasion.

All the school felt quite excited when three o'clock on Thursday afternoon arrived, and they were left to themselves in the large classroom. Big girls, little girls, new girls, and old girls sat on the forms in giggling anticipation, chattering like swallows on the eve of migration, and determined to have a good time and enjoy themselves.

"You're the eldest! Open the ball!" said Iva, pushing Nesta forward.

But Nesta had turned shy. She had never been in such a position before, and, flushing scarlet, she urged her utter inability to cope with the matter.

"I can't! You do it - or Muriel!" she whispered in an agonized voice.

But Muriel, in spite of her ambition, was also afflicted with stage-fright and passed on the honour.

Iva, making a supreme effort, called to the girls for silence, but they were too much out of hand to listen to her and only went on talking. Merle, following some wise advice administered by Mavis, had allowed the other three to have first innings, but as none seemed capable of controlling the meeting she now stepped to the front and, making a megaphone of a roll of foolscap, yelled, "Order!" with all the force of her lungs. The effect was instantaneous. There was an immediate dead hush, and all eyes were turned in her direction.

"We're here this afternoon on business, and our first matter is to elect a chairwoman," she proclaimed. "Will somebody kindly nominate one."

"I beg to propose Merle," piped Iva.

"And I beg to second her," fluttered Nesta, taking courage.

The clapping and stamping that followed witnessed the entire approval of the meeting. Merle was unanimously elected to the chair, and having thus received the symbol of authority proceeded to wield it. She was not in the least bashful, and was quite ready to cope with anything that lay before her. She held up a hand for silence and addressed her audience.

"I've told you we're here on business, and I want to explain. As it affects everybody, perhaps you'll kindly listen without talking. Will those three girls on the back bench move out here? Thanks! Now you all know the school has started on a new era, and we hope it's going to forge ahead. In the past we haven't done very much in the way of societies. Perhaps that's all the better, because it gives us the chance to make a clean start now, without any back traditions to hamper us. What I propose is this: We'll go slow at first until we get into the swing of things, and then later on we can blossom out as much as we like. I suggest that we should get up three societies:

"A Games Club.

"A Literary Club.

"An Entertainment Club.

"The Games Club will try and work up a decent hockey team, and when our play is worth anything, we'll see if we can't arrange a match with some other school. The Literary Club will run a magazine, to which you'll all be welcome to send contributions; and the Entertainment Club will concentrate on getting up theatricals or something of that sort for the end of the term. Does this meet your views?"

"Rather!"

"A1."

"Go ahead!" shouted several voices.

"Well, our first business is to appoint a president and a secretary for each. I'm going to write a few likely names upon the blackboard, and then you can make your choice. I ought to add that the boarders have already started a Recreation Club of their own, and have made Nesta Pitman president and Aubrey Simpson secretary. This has nothing to do with the day-girls, but I just mention it, thinking you'd like to know about it. We haven't time for a ballot, so if you'll propose candidates we'll take the voting by a show of hands."

An interesting and exciting ten minutes followed, in which the merits and demerits of various nominations were discussed, and the following girls were finally elected to office:

GAMES CLUB

President. Merle Ramsay.
Secretary. Kitty Trefyre.
Committee. Muriel Burnitt.
    Aubrey Simpson.
    Beata Castleton.
    Tattie Carew.
    Edith Carey.
    Peggie Morrison.

LITERARY CLUB

President. Muriel Burnitt.
Secretary and Editress of Magazine. Mavis Ramsay.
Committee. Iva Westwood.   Maude Carey.
    Merle Ramsay.   Fay Macleod.
    Nesta Pitman.   Peggie Morrison.

ENTERTAINMENTS CLUB

President. Iva Westwood.
Secretary. Nesta Pitman.
Committee. Muriel Burnitt. Aubrey Simpson.
    Mavis Ramsay. Sybil Vernon.
    Merle Ramsay. Kitty Trefyre.

It was just when the successful candidates were receiving congratulations that Beata Castleton stood up.

"As this is an open meeting may I make a suggestion?" she asked.

"Certainly," replied Merle from the chair.

"Well, I should like to suggest a 'Nature Study Club.' There doesn't seem to be anything of that sort in the school, is there?"

"We have a museum somewhere about the place, I believe," admitted Merle.

"It's all put away in boxes," said Edith.

"Then why can't we bring it out and arrange it and add to it? And can't we start a record, year by year, of when we find the first specimens of certain wild flowers, hear the first notes of certain birds, and see migratory birds? It would be ever so interesting."

"What a splendid idea! I'd like to second that!" exclaimed Mavis, jumping up in great enthusiasm.

The general feeling was in favour of the proposition, and the Nature Study Club was duly inaugurated, with Beata for president and Fay Macleod for secretary, and a committee consisting mostly of the particular little set of girls who motored daily from Chagmouth.

By four o'clock the whole of the business was concluded, the societies were established, and a very hopeful start had been made. Among the many activities of that important afternoon one point seemed to stand out firmly and clearly - Merle above all the other monitresses had shown herself capable of taking the lead. Where Iva, Nesta, and Muriel had failed to control the school she had restored order, conducted the meeting admirably, and exhibited considerable powers of organisation. She had undoubtedly justified her position, and had won the respect of most of her comrades.

"Did I do all right?" she asked Mavis anxiously, as they walked home.

"Splendiferously! I was bursting with pride! I couldn't have done it myself, Merle! When I saw all that rackety crew talking and ragging, I thought it was hopeless and that we should have to fetch Miss Mitchell. Some of those juniors had just made up their minds to give trouble. You tackled them marvellously."

"I wasn't going to give in to them!" declared Merle. "I meant to stop their ragging if I had to go round and box all their ears. Well! They know now they have to behave themselves or I'll know the reason why! But oh, Mavis! I don't think Muriel will ever forgive me for being chairwoman."

"Why not?"

"She never wanted me to be a monitress!"

"Nonsense!"

"It's the truth."

"Well, she missed her own opportunity, so she can't blame you for taking it this afternoon."

"She's against me all the same. Iva and Nesta are quite nice, but there are going to be squalls with Muriel. You'll take my part?"

"Of course I shall, through thick and thin. You can always count on your own sister."

"That's something to go upon at any rate. I shall need support. I don't believe it's going to be an easy business."

"'Uneasy lies the head that wears a crown,'" quoted Mavis laughingly.

"Exactly. I wanted tremendously to be monitress, but I didn't realise all I was in for. I see many breezes in front."

"You'll weather them all, don't fear! After such a splendid start I've every confidence in you. It's only a question now of keeping it up and going ahead."

Merle was not mistaken in her estimation of the difficulties that lay before her. A certain section of the juniors, led by Winnie Osborne and Joyce Colman, the firebrands of the Third form, offered great resistance to the authority of the monitresses, and put every possible obstacle in their way. To keep these unruly youngsters in order meant a constant clashing of wills, and needed much courage and determination. Some of the new girls also were inclined to rebel and to air their own views. Sybil Vernon, in particular, was a thorn in the flesh. She had been at boarding-school before, and on the strength of her previous experience she offered advice upon any and every occasion. She was very aggrieved that she had not been eligible for election to office herself.

"I know so much more about it than most of you!" she would explain airily. "If Miss Pollard had only chosen *me* as a monitress I could have organised everything exactly like it used to be done at The Limes."

Sybil was a curious girl, fair, with a fat babyish face, and a vast idea of her own importance. She was very proud of her family, and never for a moment forgot, or allowed anybody else to forget, that she belonged to the Vernons of Renshaw Court, and that Sir Richard Vernon was her second cousin. She expected a great deal more attention than the school was willing to accord to her, and was invariably offended or aggrieved or annoyed about something. The girls did not take her very seriously, and laughed at what they called her 'jim-jams,' which had the effect of making her first very indignant and finally reducing her to floods of tears.

Though Sybil might be annoying there was really not much harm in her, and her criticisms were very easily combated. A different girl altogether, however, was Kitty Trefyre. She also had been at another school, and set forth standards of conduct which were dissimilar from those at 'The Moorings.' She was cautious in airing these, and wisely so, for most of them caused the monitresses to lift their eyebrows in amazement, whereupon she would instantly retract her remarks and declare she was only 'ragging.' How much she really meant Merle never knew, but the latter did not trust her.

"There's a sneaky look about her eyes," she commented to Mavis. "Sybil lunges out and finds open fault, but Kitty hits in the dark. I hope she's not going to spoil Iva!"

"Oh, don't say that!"

"They're chums already, and Iva is rather a chameleon! She takes the colour of her character from her friends."

CHAPTER IV

CHAGMOUTH FOLK

As this book partly concerns the doings of the group of girls who came daily from Chagmouth to Durracombe, we will follow them as they motored back on their ten miles' journey from school. Squashed together in 'the sardine-tin,' as they irreverently nicknamed the highly respectable car driven by Mr. Vicary, who owned the garage close to the mill, they held high jinks and talked at least thirteen to the dozen. There was so much to discuss. The school was new to all of them, and naturally they wished to criticise its methods, its teachers, its girls, and its prospects of fun during the ensuing term.

"I like Miss Mitchell!"

"Yes, she's jolly, though I fancy she could be stern."

"Oh, I shouldn't like to face her in the study, of course."

"Miss Fanny is a dear!"

"And so is Miss Pollard."

"What d'you think of the monitresses?"

"Merle is A1!"

"Yes, I'm taken with Mavis and Merle! Partly because they

seem to belong to Chagmouth. They come over nearly every Saturday with Dr. Tremayne."

"Good! Then we shall see something of them. Hello! What's this car trying to pass us? Babbie Williams! I'd forgotten for the moment she lives at Chagmouth too."

It was Babbie, driving in solitary state, who flew by in the big motor, which turned up the side road that led to The Warren. She gave a friendly nod as she passed, and the six 'sardines' smiled in return.

"It's a case of 'we are seven' from Chagmouth," commented Fay. "If we include Mavis and Merle that would make nine. I guess we'll get up a set of nature study rambles on Saturday afternoons and all go out together. We'd have some real frolics!"

"Rather! I'm your girl! Romola and I are ready for any fun that's going. That's to say if there's going to be time for any fun. But with all the pile of lessons Miss Mitchell has given us we shall be busy, with our noses at the grindstone. It always takes both of us hours to do our prep!"

The car meanwhile, with Mr. Vicary at the driving-wheel, had run across the moor and down the steep hill, and was jolting over the cobble-stones of the narrow main street of Chagmouth. It stopped outside the Post Office, for the principal reason that if it went any farther it would be impossible for it to turn round, and the girls, dismounting, took their satchels or piles of books, said good-bye to one another, and scattered to their respective homes. Beata and Romola crossed the bridge that spanned the brook, skirted the harbour, climbed a flight of steps cut in the solid rock, and reached a house which stood on the top of a high crag overlooking the sea. It was an ideal spot for an artist to live, and it was chiefly for its glorious view that Mr. Castleton had chosen it. He was intensely sensitive to his surroundings, and preferred a picturesque cottage, however inconvenient, to the comforts of an unaesthetic, bow-windowed, modern, red-brick, suburban residence.

"Romance before everything!" he declared. "It's impossible to paint unless you're in the right atmosphere. English scenery is getting spoilt and vulgarised to such a degree that there'll soon be none of it left to sketch. Where are the beautiful villages of thirty years ago? Gone - most of them! The thatched roofs replaced by corrugated iron, and the hedges clipped close to please the motorists. I defy anybody to make a successful picture out of a clipped hedge! Even the gnarled apple trees are being cut down and replaced by market gardeners' 'choice saplings.' Picturesque England will soon be a thing of the past! I consider Chagmouth one of the last strongholds for an artist, and I'm going to live here as long as it remains unspoilt. There's enough work to keep me busy for several years at any rate."

It is part of an artist's business to move about from place to place in quest of fresh subjects. Mr. Castleton had spent some years at Porthkeverne, and having, from a professional point of view, exhausted that neighbourhood, he had transferred himself and his family to a new horizon. He had a genius for discovering his right niche, and he had been fortunate enough to light upon exactly the place that appealed to him. It would not have suited everybody. It was a long low house, made of three fishermen's cottages thrown into one, built so close to the edge of the cliff that it seemed like a sea-bird's nest, with windows overlooking the channel and the harbour, and a strip of stony garden behind. Inside, the accommodation was somewhat cramped, but the rooms, if small, were quaint, with an old-fashioned air about the panelled parlour and raftered dining-room that suggested bygone days of smugglers and privateers. Below, in a nook of the cliff, stood an old sail-shed, which Mr. Castleton had turned into his studio. The big new skylight had only just been fitted into the roof, and the stove which was to heat it during the winter was still at Durracombe station waiting for the carrier to fetch it, but canvases were already hung round the walls, the throne was erected and the big easel placed in position, and an old fisherman, with weather-beaten countenance and picturesque stained jersey, sat every morning for his portrait.

Those of our readers who have met the Castletons before in *The Head Girl at the Gables*, will remember that they were a very large family. Morland, the eldest, had been at the war, had won the D.C.M., and was now learning engineering; Claudia was studying singing in London; Madox had been sent for his first term at boarding-school; and the four little ones, Constable, Lilith, Perugia, and Gabriel, were still in the nursery. There was only one gap. Landry, poor Landry, who had never been like other boys, had passed over the divide and joined the beautiful mother whom in features he had so strongly resembled. A painting of him, as a little child in her arms, hung on the studio wall. In some respects it was the most brilliant portrait which Mr. Castleton had ever achieved. He always showed it to visitors as a specimen of his best work.

At the time this story begins, Beata and Romola were fourteen and thirteen years of age. They thoroughly maintained the family reputation for good looks. There was a certain resemblance between them, and yet a difference. Beata's eyes were clear grey, with dark lines round the iris, and her hair was the exact shade of one of her father's best English gold picture frames. She was a clever, capable girl, with a great love for music, and was beginning to play the violin rather well. She got on quite tolerably with her stepmother, and was fond of the little half-brothers and sisters, though the warmest corner of her heart was reserved for Madox, who was the baby of the elder portion of the family.

Romola, blue-eyed and ethereal, with long amber hair like a Saxon princess, was her father's favourite model whenever he wished to depict scenes of olden times. She figured as 'Guinevere' in a series of illustrations to the *Morte d'Arthur*, as 'Elaine' her portrait had been exhibited in the Academy, as 'The Lady of Shalott' she had appeared in a coloured frontispiece of *The Art Review*, she inspired a most successful poster of 'Cinderella,' and was the original of a series of fairy drawings in a children's annual. She was not so clever or go-ahead as Beata, and was rather dreamy and romantic in temperament, with a gift towards painting and poetry, and a disinclination to do anything very definite. She left most of the problems of life to Beata, and seldom troubled to make decisions for herself. She was rather a pet with Violet, her young stepmother, who, while preferring her to her sister, found her the less useful of the two.

"You go, Beata, you're so quick!" Violet would say, when she wanted an errand done, and for the same reason gave the charge of the children to the one who was the more capable of assuming the responsibility.

It was not that Romola consciously shirked home duties, but she would any time rather pose for an hour on the throne in the studio than take temporary command of the nursery. Beata, on the contrary, hated sitting still, and considered there was no greater penance than to be commandeered by her father as a model. Her energetic temperament liked to find its expression in outdoor activities. She had set to work upon the neglected garden, and was busy trying to make flower-beds, and she looked forward keenly to the forthcoming hockey season at school. The daily drive to Durracombe and back was pure delight, and formed her greatest compensation for leaving Porthkeverne and The Gables.

The Haven, as the house occupied by the Castletons was called, had been changed into its present form by an old retired sea-captain, and there was much about it that suggested a nautical atmosphere. The panelled walls of the parlour might have been taken from a ship's cabin, the dining-room contained convenient lockers, there was a small observatory upstairs built to accommodate a big telescope, and the figure-head of a vessel adorned the garden. Young Mrs. Castleton, whose tastes inclined towards up-to-date comforts, often grumbled at its inconveniences, but on the whole the family liked it. They would not have exchanged it for a suburban villa for worlds. Just on the opposite side of the harbour, with the jetty and the broad strip of green water in between, was the furnished house rented at present by the Macleods. It stood in the more aristocratic portion of Chagmouth, apart from the town and the fishing, in company with one or two other newly-built residences. It was charmingly pretty and artistic, in a perfectly modern fashion, and had been designed by a famous architect. Its owner, a retired naval officer, had gone abroad for a year, and had let the place in his absence, rejoicing to have secured a careful tenant. He might certainly congratulate himself upon leaving his house in such good hands. Mr. Macleod was an American gentleman, who, owing to a nervous breakdown, was travelling in Europe, and happening in the course of the summer to wander to Chagmouth, he had fallen in love with the quaint old town and had decided to spend the winter there. The factor which largely influenced this decision was the presence of Mr. Castleton. Mr. Macleod was an enthusiastic amateur painter, and the prospect of being able to take lessons from so good an artist was sufficient to chain him to Chagmouth. His wife encouraged the idea.

"George is just miserable if he's nothing to do," she explained to her friends. "The doctor told me not to let him read too much or take up any special mental hobby, but sketching strikes the happy medium. He thoroughly enjoys pottering about in Mr. Castleton's studio, or making drawings down on the quay. It's not arduous work and yet it keeps him occupied. I like the house, and Fay can go to school near, so I expect we're fixed here until next spring at any rate. If I get too bored I shall run over to Paris and see my sister, but really I haven't been well lately myself, and it will do me good to take a thorough rest for a while."

Fay, who had formed an enthusiastic friendship with Beata and Romola, was as pleased with Chagmouth as her parents. From the windows of Bella Vista she could look across the harbour to The Haven, and had already arranged a code of signals by which she might communicate with her chums. She was a bright, amusing girl, rather grown-up for her age, and the constant companion of her father and mother.

"Fay runs the house!" Mrs. Macleod would declare sometimes; but she was immensely proud of her young daughter, and unwilling to thwart her in any of the projects which she might care to take up. These, indeed, were many. Fay dabbled in numerous hobbies, and her demands varied from photographic materials to special sandals for toe dancing. She thoroughly enjoyed life, and the freshness of her enthusiasm provided her parents with a perpetual interest. To those friends who urged boarding-school her mother was ready with the reply:

"Why must we be parted from her? She's her father's best tonic! She keeps him young and makes him laugh. She's getting her education and living her home life at the same time, and that seems to me ideal. We shall probably have to spare her later on to be married, so we may as well make the most of her now while we've got her. It's the chief tragedy of parents that the children grow up and go away. We'll enjoy our nest while we have our one chick here. When the young ones are fledged, the old birds stop singing."

Of the other girls who shared the car to Durracombe, Tattie Carew, whose parents were in India had come to live with her aunt Miss Grant, in the ivy-covered house at the top of the hill, while Nan and Lizzie Colville were the daughters of the newly-appointed vicar. All six, therefore, were fresh comers to the neighbourhood, and as yet had neither explored the whole of its beauties nor learnt to understand its traditions. In both of these respects Mavis and Merle, though non-residents, had the advantage of them. Their friendship with Bevis Talland, the boy who, once the village foundling, had turned out to be heir to the Chagmouth estate, had given them an intimate acquaintance with the life of the place. Bevis had shown them the haunts of the birds, and the best places for wild flowers, had told them the local legends and the histories of the various worthies of the parish. The little town indeed seemed strangely empty without him, but at present he was away at school, and later would be going to college, though eventually, when he came of age, he would probably take up his residence in the old family home. The Warren, where Tallands had lived for so many generations, had been let on a lease to Mr. Glyn Williams, and the lawyers who managed the property had decided that this arrangement should be continued during Bevis's minority; heavy death duties and land-taxes would cripple the estate for some years, and it was not worth while running a house for the sake of a schoolboy who could pass only his holidays there. Mr. Glyn Williams meanwhile had bought Bodoran Hall near Port Sennen, and would have leisure to make all the many structural alterations which he wished before he was obliged to leave The Warren. Through Bevis's foster-mother, Mrs. Penruddock of Grimbal's Farm, where Dr. Tremayne had his branch surgery at Chagmouth, Mavis and Merle were also kept very much in touch with the tone of the place and knew most of the little happenings that occurred. They were friendly with many of the village people, almost all of whom were their uncle's patients at one time or another, and the Saturday expedition over the moor from Durracombe was to them the central attraction of the whole week.

On the first Saturday afternoon of the new term, by special invitation, they called at The Haven, and made the acquaintance of at least a portion of the Castleton family. Beata was practising her violin, but she laid it aside at once.

"I'll finish my half-hour afterwards. It will do quite as well this evening. It's too fine a day to stay stuffing inside the house. Do you care to come into the garden? We can step out through this window. These are the babies, Constable, Lilith, Perugia, and Gabriel. I was keeping an eye on them while I practised, to see they weren't in any mischief. Violet has a headache and is lying down. She's our stepmother, you know. We don't let the little ones call her Violet though! Come here, Perugia, and shake hands! She's rather a pet, isn't she?"

The younger Castletons, from curly-headed Constable, known

familiarly as 'Cooney,' to lovely three-year-old Baby Gabriel, were beautiful children, and looked particularly picturesque in holland play-overalls embroidered with saxe-blue. Mr. Castleton, who valued artistic effect before everything, found Constable one of his most useful models, and though the boy was now seven and a half, he was generally dressed in a Kate Greenaway smock and his crop of golden curls was still uncut.

"Don't touch him!" his father would protest, whenever the question of Constable's hair arose in the family; "as he is he's worth an income to me! He always gets into exhibitions and he generally sells. He's just what the average British patron wants to buy. The public can't always understand my allegorical pictures, but they know a pretty child when they see one. He'll be spoilt for the studio if he loses his curls, and I want to sketch him as a singing angel, and as a water-baby, and for some of my Hans Andersen illustrations. It's too bad to ruin his artistic value just when I've trained him to pose properly. It will be years before Gabriel learns to sit as still - if he ever does."

The little fellow had charmingly attractive manners, and came forward willingly to talk to visitors. He and Perugia were the talkative ones; Lilith, a flaxen-haired fairy of six, was very shy, and the baby was busy with his own affairs and refused to be interrupted.

"Romola is sitting for Father," explained Beata. "I expect he'd let her go now though, if you'd care to come for a walk with us. Bother! What shall I do with the little ones? I can't leave them to Violet when she's lying down."

"Bring them with you," suggested Mavis, who was making friends with Perugia.

"Should you mind? I'll tell you what! I'll borrow the donkey from the farm, then they can ride in turns and won't get tired. Mrs. Donnithorne is very good-natured about lending it. Constable, you run and ask her, while we go to fetch Romola.

Do you care to come to the studio?"

Mavis and Merle were only too delighted to have the opportunity of taking a peep into Mr. Castleton's den, so followed Beata to the old sail-room down a flight of steps cut in the cliff side. They remembered the place, for Job Helyar used to plait osiers there, and they had come once to buy a basket from him. In its former days it had been nothing but a rough shed. They hardly recognised it now it was turned into a studio. Beata went boldly in, and introduced her visitors. Her father was painting a study of Romola for incorporation in a large historical picture. She was standing on the throne, in a beautiful scarlet mediaeval costume, with her long fair hair unbound and flowing like an amber waterfall down her back. Mr. Castleton did not look at all pleased at being interrupted in his work, but he glanced at his watch and nodded a reluctant permission to Romola to relieve her pose. She came down from the platform, stretching her tired arms.

"I'm supposed to be holding up a casket, and it's a horrid position to keep," she explained. "May I go now, Dad? We want Mavis and Merle to take us for a walk. I shan't be three seconds changing out of this costume. You think the study is like me, Mavis? Show them the sketch for the picture, Dad! Now you see where my place will be in it - just there. The little page-boy is Constable, and Violet sat for the queen."

While Romola slipped off her mediaeval robe and plaited her long hair, Beata escorted the visitors back to the garden. She fetched a pair of field-glasses, took a survey through them, then declared:

"I can see Fay at her window, and Tattie sitting on the bank above her aunt's tennis-court. I'll signal to them both, and they'll meet us by the bridge. We'll call at the Vicarage and pick up Nan and Lizzie, then we shall be quite a jolly party. Oh, here's Constable with Billy. I'm so glad Mrs. Donnithorne will lend him to us. Are we all ready? Then come along!"

The six picturesque Castletons were already well known in the streets of Chagmouth, and many eyes were turned to look at them as they passed along, with Perugia and Gabriel riding the donkey together, Romola holding them both on, and Lilith leading Billy by the bridle. Kindly comments came from cottage doorways.

"Stick on tight, ma dear!"

"Don't 'ee walk behind or her'll kick!"

"Mind her don't run away with ee!"

"Don't they ride pretty, bless 'em!"

At the bridge by the harbour the party was reinforced by Fay and Tattie, and farther on they were joined by the Colvilles, so that they were twelve strong as they left the town, and a particularly merry crew. At the beginning of the first hill, however, the donkey stopped dead. Several hands seized its bridle and tried to urge it forward, while Mavis and Merle pushed it in the rear, but not all their efforts could induce it to stir an inch.

"Romola! What utter idiots we are!" exclaimed Beata. "Of course we've forgotten the peppermints!"

"Bother! So we have! We must go back for some, that's all!"

"The 'donk' won't go without peppermints! He simply loves them!" explained Beata tragically.

"We always take a big packet of them with us to give him. He expects them! He's turning his head round to look for them!"

"Bless his heart, he shall have them then!" cooed Merle, patting the dusty coat of their steed. "His auntie will go and get some for him herself if he'll wait like a good boy. Is he particular what kind he gets?"

"He likes those big brown humbugs!"

"Right-o! I'll run to Denham's shop and buy some. It's not far. Wait for me, won't you?"

"Wait!" echoed Beata. "There'll be no question of going on. Nothing but humbugs will make him move his four feet. We'll camp here till you come back."

Merle performed her errand quickly, returning with two packets of sweets, one for Billy and the other for the rest of the party. The donkey, after consuming several peppermints, condescended to move on, and the procession started once more. They had not gone far, however, before a mishap occurred: in lieu of saddle a cushion had been tied on to Billy's back, the strap had loosened, the cushion suddenly slipped, and Perugia and Gabriel descended into the road. Romola managed to break their fall, but they were both terrified, and refused to mount again, so Constable took a turn instead, holding the bridle himself, while Lilith, with all the Castleton instinct for artistic effect, gathered posies of wild flowers and wove them into a wreath for the donkey's neck.

The small people could not walk fast, and the steed stopped so often to demand refreshments, that the expedition was very leisurely and they did not proceed far. They had only reached the point above the lighthouse when Mavis, with an eye on her wrist watch, declared it was time to turn back.

"We'll go with you another time, when we haven't to trail all this crew along!" sighed Beata, as she bade good-bye to her friends. "Children are a nuisance if you want to get on quickly. I'd have left them in the garden if I could! Come and see us again at The Haven, won't you? I wish Claudia and Morland were at home and we'd have some music. Well, I shall see you next week, I suppose. I'm to have my first violin lesson on Monday. I don't know whether I'm glad or not. I expect I shall be terrified of Mr. Barlow. I learnt from a lady before. How I'm going to practise and do all the home lessons Miss

Mitchell sets us I can't imagine! I think I shall strike like the 'donk' and refuse to stir unless they give me peppermints!"

CHAPTER V

MISS MITCHELL, B.A.

Naturally at present the most prominent person at 'The Moorings' was Miss Mitchell. Hers was a task which required a combination of a number of very high qualities. It needed force of character and tact, initiative and patience, energy and experience. To reorganise an old school is a far more difficult matter than to start an entirely new one, especially when those responsible for the former *regime* have not absolutely retired. To a certain extent the Misses Pollard had given their teacher a free hand, but she realised that at first it would be wise to go slowly and not make the changes too drastic. She did not yet know what stuff she had to work upon, the characters or capacities of her pupils, or their readiness to adopt her ideas. While leading the school, she wished it to be self-developing, that is to say, she thought it better to give the girls a few general directions, and allow them to run their own societies, than to arrange all such matters for them.

"Never mind if they make a few mistakes," she said to Miss Fanny, who held up her hands in horror at some of the names chosen to serve on committees. "If a secretary proves inefficient, the others will very soon call her a 'slacker,' and she will have to reform or resign. It will be a question of public opinion. A girl may shirk her lessons in school and her classmates don't much care, but if she shirks the work she has undertaken to do for a society they will be very indignant. These clubs are an elementary object-lesson in community life,

Angela Brazil

and will teach that each individual must do something for the general good. The girls must 'feel their feet' before they can run; they'll probably have difficulties but they'll learn by experience, and in the meantime they'll be shaping their own traditions."

"Ye-es; I suppose you're right," dubiously agreed Miss Fanny, whose ideal of management was to trust everything in the hands of a few girls whom she knew best and discourage any signs of individuality on the part of the others.

As regards the work of the various forms Miss Mitchell, helped by her assistant mistress Miss Barnes, made many innovations. She introduced new subjects and fresh modes of teaching, and fixed a very high standard of efficiency. She expected great concentration, and exacted hard work, especially in the matter of home preparation, but she was an exceedingly interesting teacher and put much enthusiasm into her lessons. She had a theory that no subject was really absorbed unless it was vividly realised by the pupils.

"Imagination is half the value of education" was her favourite saying. "A child may reel off a string of facts, but unless it can apply them they are undigested mental food and of no use. What I want to do is to find out how far each girl understands what she has learnt. Mere parrot repetition is quite valueless in my opinion, and most public examinations are little better."

Miss Mitchell's method of testing the knowledge of her pupils was undoubtedly modern. She would teach them certain episodes of history, explaining particularly the characters of the various personages and the motives for their actions, then, instead of a verbal or written catechism on the lesson, she would make the girls act the scene, using their own words, and trying as far as possible to reproduce the atmosphere of the period. Free criticism was allowed afterwards, and any anachronisms, such as tea in the times of Queen Elizabeth, or tobacco during the Wars of the Roses, were carefully pointed out. Most of the girls liked this new method immensely. It encouraged their dramatic instincts, and resembled impromptu theatricals. It was a point of honour to throw themselves thoroughly into the parts, and they would often prepare themselves at home by reading up various points in histories or encyclopaedias. This was exactly what Miss Mitchell aimed at.

"They're educating themselves!" she explained to Miss Fanny. "They'll never forget these facts that they have taken the trouble to find out. Once a girl has realised the outlook of Mary Queen of Scots or Elizabeth, and has learnt to impersonate her without glaring mistakes, she has the keynote to the history of the times. When she has spoken to 'Darnley,' 'Black Both-well,' 'Rizzio,' 'John Knox,' or to 'Bacon,' 'Raleigh,' 'Essex,' and 'Sidney,' she has turned mere names into real personages, and will be no more likely to confuse them than to mix up her friends. By supplying her own dialogue she shows exactly how much she knows of the character, and I am able to judge how far the lesson has been assimilated. Fifteen years hence I venture to think Scottish Mary or Queen Elizabeth will still be vivid remembrances to her; but would she be able to tell the date of the battle of Pinkie? And would it be of very vital importance whether she did or not? In my opinion to grasp the main motives of history and to follow the evolution of the British nation is far more necessary than memorising dates. Of course, a few must be insisted on, or there would be no means of relative comparison, but these few, accurately learnt, are better than a number repeated glibly without any particular conception of their importance."

In the teaching of geography Miss Mitchell also put her theories into action. As taught in many schools she thought it was a wearisome subject.

"You don't want to knock into a child's head the names of the capes and bays of Africa or the population of Canada, but you want to give it some conception of the different countries on the face of God's earth. Instead of making it learn the exports of Italy, show it pictures of the orange groves and of gathering the olives, and it will name you the exports for itself.

Geography ought to be as interesting as a game."

And so indeed she contrived to make it. She had brought a magic lantern to school with her, and used it for most of her lessons, arranging thick curtains to darken the windows. She had a selection of good slides showing many different countries, and when her pupils were somewhat accustomed to these she would test their knowledge by exhibiting one and asking them where it was, whether in a hot or cold country, what kind of people lived in such a place, what fruits, flowers, and animals would be found there, and for what reasons British traders went to it. If the girls made mistakes she would show them again the particular slides relating to the place, explaining where they had been wrong, and taking them, by means of the eye, on a short foreign tour.

"Imagine you're there and you'll feel quite travellers!" she would say. "Now on this slide you notice a little pathway up the hill among some trees. If you could walk up that path what would you be likely to find? What language would the people, whom you met, speak? And how would they be dressed?"

Geography on these lines became very attractive, and, as in the case of the history lessons, the girls eagerly looked out all kinds of points in books of reference so as to come to class armed with information about the birds, flowers, or native customs of some particular country. By visualising the place, imagining themselves to be there, and relating all they saw, they created such vivid mental pictures that they could almost believe they had spent the hour really in Africa or South America, as the case might be.

"You'd know what clothes to take with you to India or Canada at any rate," said Miss Mitchell, "and what sort of a life you must be prepared to live there. Before the term is over I think you'll realise what British women are doing all over the globe. Climatic conditions have an immense effect upon people and ought to be properly understood. The knowledge of these is the foundation of the brotherhood of races."

It was not only in history and geography that Miss Mitchell made innovations. French also was to be on a different method. It had always been a successful subject at 'The Moorings,' though it had developed along old-fashioned lines. Mademoiselle Chavasse, however, had left, and the new Mademoiselle came from a very up-to-date School of Languages in London. She taught largely by the oral system, making her pupils repeat words and build them into sentences, like babies learning to talk. She used English as little as possible, trying to make them catch ideas in French without the medium of translation. Thus, in a beginners' class she would hold up a book and say, "le livre," then placing it *on* the table or *under* the table would extend her sentence to show the use of the prepositions. The girls soon began to grasp the method, and learnt to reply in French to simple questions asked them, and were given by degrees a larger vocabulary and encouraged to try to express themselves, however imperfectly, in the foreign tongue. She also instituted French games, and set the whole school singing, "Qui passe ce chemin si tard?" or "Sur le pont d'Avignon," while several of the Fifth form who could write letters in French were put into correspondence with schoolgirls in France.

Miss Pollard and Miss Fanny, who had gasped a little at some of the drastic changes, were pleased with the improvement in the teaching of French, and still more so with the innovations with regard to music. This had been a very special subject at St. Cyprian's College, where Miss Mitchell had been educated, and she was anxious to introduce some of the leading features. Her theory was that most girls learn to play the piano, a few practise the violin, but hardly any are taught to understand and appreciate music, apart from their own often unskilful performances. She arranged, therefore, to hold a weekly class at which a short lecture would be given on the works of some famous composers, with musical illustrations. A few of the selections could be played by the pupils themselves or by Miss Fanny, and others could be rendered by a gramophone. The main object was to make the girls familiar with the best compositions and cultivate their musical taste.

"Constant listening is the only way to learn appreciation," said Miss Mitchell. "You form a taste for literature by reading the best authors, not by trying to write poetry yourself! Learning an instrument is a good training, but certainly only a part of music - to understand it and criticise it is quite another matter."

So all the school, including even the little girls, met to listen to the masterpieces of Beethoven, Chopin, or Schubert, and were encouraged to note particular points and to discuss them intelligently.

"At the end of the term," said Miss Mitchell, "we'll have a concert, just among ourselves, and then I hope some of you will surprise me. You must all practise hard, because it will be a great honour to be asked to play on that particular afternoon."

In revising the curriculum of 'The Moorings' upon these very modern lines, Miss Mitchell did not neglect the athletic side. The school did not yet possess a gymnasium, but there were classes for drill and calisthenics, and games were compulsory.

"A good thing too!" commented Merle. "Some of the girls are fearful slackers! They've never been accustomed to stir themselves. Maude Carey hardly knows how to run. I believe she thinks it's unladylike! And Nesta would shirk if she could. Those kids need a fearful amount of coaching. I shall have my work cut out with them."

Merle, owing to her enthusiasm for sports, had been chosen as Games Captain, and was doing her best to cultivate a proper enthusiasm for hockey in the school. In this matter she had the full co-operation of the new mistress. Merle liked Miss Mitchell, whose cheery, breezy, practical ways particularly appealed to her. Merle was not given to violent affections, especially for teachers, so this attraction was almost a matter of first love. She, who had never minded blame at school, found herself caring tremendously for praise in class. It raised the standard of her work enormously. She could do very well if she tried. She had always poked fun at girls who took much trouble over home lessons, and had been accustomed to leave her own till the last possible moment. It was certainly a new phase to find her getting out her books immediately after tea, or practising for half an hour before breakfast. She was ready to do anything to win notice from Miss Mitchell, and was decidedly jealous that Iva and Nesta, being boarders, were able to see more of her, and thus establish a greater intimacy. Merle always wanted to 'go one better' than the other monitresses. The status of all four was exactly equal, and so far there was no head girl at 'The Moorings.' Merle had indeed taken a most prominent part at the general meeting of the school, but though she might be the unacknowledged leader, that gave her no increased authority. Sometimes her excess of zeal led to ructions. Miss Mitchell had strongly urged the necessity of improving the games, and particularly of training the juniors to play hockey properly. Merle seized upon them at every opportunity and made them practise. One afternoon, as everybody filed out at four o'clock, she captured her recruits and began some instruction. But unfortunately it happened that Winnie and Joyce, who were her aptest pupils, were wanted by Nesta for schemes of her own, and she came and called them in.

"Can't spare them now!" objected Merle briefly.

"Sorry! But they'll have to come!"

"Not if their Games Captain wants them!"

"I'm their hostel monitress!"

"Miss Mitchell asked me to see to the hockey!"

"Then you must get day-girls to stay for your practice. I've instructions to see that all the boarders come straight back to the hostel after school!"

Merle gave way with a very bad grace. She felt that Nesta was interfering out of sheer officiousness.

"What a jack-in-office!" she grumbled under her breath. "I believe those boarders may do anything they like until tea-time. Nesta needn't plume herself upon being prime favourite with Miss Mitchell. She may whisk Joyce and Winnie off now and spoil our practice, but I'll be even with her in some other way!"

In talking about the various school institutions, Miss Mitchell mentioned one day that there ought to be a general record of the various societies and their officers, and the work which they had undertaken to do.

"It should be kept in the study so as to be available any time for reference," she said. "It would be a far simpler method than having to ask the secretaries for particulars."

This gave Merle an idea. She said nothing to her fellow-monitresses, but she at once began to compile the list which Miss Mitchell wanted. She was determined to do it beautifully. Her handwriting was not remarkably good, so she decided to type it. There was a little typewriter in Uncle David's consulting-room, which he allowed her to use, and though she was so far from being an adept at it that it actually took her longer than using pen and ink, she thought the result would justify the trouble. She meant to stitch the sheets together and fasten them inside a cardboard cover, decorated with an artistic design. She set to work upon it with much energy and enthusiasm.

She was leaving school one afternoon when Muriel Burnitt ran up to her.

"By the by, Merle! Can you give me the names of the committee of the Nature Club? I can't just remember them all."

"What d'you want them for?" asked Merle suspiciously.

"Oh, to write out for Miss Mitchell! She was asking for a list the other day."

"Fay Macleod is secretary of the Nature Club. She'd be able to tell you exactly," temporised Merle.

"So she would! I'll ask her to-morrow."

Merle went home with her head in a whirl. It was quite evident that Muriel had hit upon exactly the same idea as herself, and intended to present Miss Mitchell with a full record of the societies.

"Only, hers will probably be written in an exercise-book and not be half as nice as mine! She mustn't forestall me, though! However artistic my list is, it will fall very flat if Muriel gives hers in first. I've got to finish it somehow to-night and take it to school to-morrow morning. That's certain!"

When Merle made up her mind about anything, nothing could move her. Directly she got home she set to work upon the book-back, and toiled away at it, utterly ignoring her preparation. In vain Mavis urged the claims of Latin verbs and Shakespeare recitation.

"I shan't stop till I've finished this!" declared Merle stubbornly. "Not if I sit up all night over it. Bother the old 'Merchant of Venice' and beastly Latin verbs! I'll glance through them at breakfast-time and trust to luck. Surely Miss Mitchell will understand when she knows how busy I've been over this! I shall give it to her before nine o'clock."

"Can't I help you? I've finished my prep."

"No, thanks! I want it to be entirely my own work."

Merle was not so clever at drawing as Mavis, but she contrived to turn out a very pretty cover all the same. She illuminated 'The Moorings' in large letters upon it, and painted a picture of a boat moored to a jetty below, as being an appropriate design. She stitched the typed sheets, fastened the whole together, and tied it with a piece of saxe-blue ribbon (saxe was emphatically Miss Mitchell's pet colour), then she printed upon the back of it, 'With much love from your affectionate pupil Merle Ramsay.' She sat up over it long after Mavis and Aunt Nellie had gone to bed, and, indeed, finished it hurriedly under the eyes of Jessop, who was waiting to turn out the gas.

"Can't I just look over my Latin?" implored Merle.

"Not a word!" declared the old servant. "Put those books away, Miss Merle, and go upstairs. We'll be having you with brain-fever at this rate! I don't approve of all these home lessons. Why can't they teach you what they want to in school, I should like to know? That's what teachers are paid for, isn't it? I've no patience with this continual writing in the evenings. A nice bit of sewing would be more to my mind. You've not done more than an inch of that crochet pattern I taught you. Being monitress is all very well, I daresay, but I'm not going to let you sit up till midnight, my dearie, over your books. Not if I have to go myself to Miss Pollard, and tell her my mind about it."

Merle had meant to wake up a little earlier and run through her preparation, but she was sleepier than usual next morning, and had to be roused by Mavis. She opened her eyes most unwillingly.

"I never heard Jessop bring the hot water. It can't be half-past seven! Oh, bother! I'd give all the world to be left quiet in bed! Go away!"

"All right! Stop in bed, and let Muriel give her list to Miss Mitchell!" said Mavis.

Whereupon Merle groaned, sat up, and began to pull on her stockings.

"Guess I'll take the wind out of Muriel's sails!" she murmured.

The list was beautifully wrapped up in a sheet of new tissue-paper, and Merle carried it proudly to school. Miss Mitchell was generally in the study from about 8.45 till 9 o'clock, so there would be nice time to present it before call-over. On this particular morning, however, as fate would have it, the study was unoccupied. Merle peeped in many times, went to the hostel, asked the boarders if they had seen Miss Mitchell, but was utterly unable to find her. She seemed to have mysteriously disappeared, and only walked in, from no one knew where, just in time to take the register. The Fifth form marched away to its classroom, and Merle's offering, for the present, was obliged to be consigned to the recesses of her desk.

Latin was the first lesson, and as far as she was concerned it was a dismal failure. Miss Mitchell looked surprised at her ghastly mistakes, and one or two of the girls glanced at each other. Merle was hot and flustered at the close of the hour, and closed her books with relief. She hoped to manage a little better in 'The Merchant of Venice,' which was at least an English subject. The girls were supposed to learn the notes, and were questioned upon them and upon the meaning of the passages, and she trusted to native wit and successful guessing to supply her answers. The teacher, however, very soon grasped the fact that Merle knew nothing about the lesson, asked her to recite, and found that she broke down at the end of three lines.

"You're absolutely unprepared!" said Miss Mitchell scathingly. "A nice example for a monitress to set to the rest of the form! Come to the study at eleven, and report yourself! I'm astonished at you, Merle!"

A very depressed and humiliated monitress entered the study at 'interval' to receive her scolding.

"I can't understand you! You have been doing so well. Why

have you suddenly slacked off?" asked her inquisitor, who believed in getting to the bottom of things if a girl shirked her work.

Merle, who was too much upset even to mention her reason, and who had left the offering inside her desk, said nothing, and only looked unutterably miserable. Matters, therefore, were at rather a deadlock, when there was a tap at the door and Mavis entered bearing the precious parcel.

"Miss Mitchell, *please*! In case Merle won't tell, I've brought this. She sat up fearfully late last night doing it for you, and that's why she didn't do her prep. Please excuse me for coming in!" and Mavis bolted in much confusion.

Miss Mitchell unwrapped the parcel and looked critically at its contents.

"It's very kind of you to have made this for me, Merle," she said, in a gentler voice. "I only wish it hadn't been at the expense of your preparation. I like the monitresses to do all they can for the school, but they must remember their own work comes first, and that they have to set an example to the rest. Don't let a thing like this happen again! I thought you would have had more discretion. The list could have waited a day or two. I was not in such a hurry for it as all that. It was kindly meant, but a little excess of zeal, wasn't it? Thank you for it all the same! There! I'll put it on my desk so that it will be always ready if I want to refer to it. Now run along, or you won't have time to eat your lunch before the bell rings."

Merle, hurrying to the dressing-room, inwardly congratulated herself.

"I got jolly well out of a bad business!" she thought. "Miss Mitchell wasn't very cross after all, and she liked the list! I've got mine in before Muriel's anyway, and it's going to stay on her desk, so she'll always have something of mine right under her eyes. She fingered that saxe-blue ribbon rather lovingly! It exactly matches her sports coat! I'll make her a calendar for Christmas and put the same kind of ribbon to hang it up by. But I don't mean to tell a single soul, in case Muriel goes and does the same! Miss Mitchell is my property, not hers!"

Angela Brazil

CHAPTER VI

FISHERMAIDENS

Several Saturdays turned out wet, and it was not until the middle of October that Mavis and Merle were again able to motor with Dr. Tremayne to Chagmouth.

They had made arrangements for a nature ramble, so, after an early lunch at Grimbal's Farm, they went to the trysting-place by the harbour to meet the other members of the club. Beata and Romola turned up alone to-day, unencumbered by younger brothers and sisters or the donkey. They had brought businesslike baskets with them, and were armed with note-books to record specimens, some apples and nuts, and a couple of log-lines.

"We might be able to get some fishing!" they explained eagerly. "Father went out yesterday in old Mr. Davis's boat, and he brought home the most *lovely* mackerel. Wouldn't it be a surprise if we could get some for ourselves? I don't see why we shouldn't!"

The idea appealed to the others. Fish were undoubtedly a division of zoology and ought to be included in their nature study. Specimens would be no less scientifically interesting from the fact that they could be eaten afterwards. Fay instantly rushed into Helyar's General Store to buy a log-line of her own; Mavis and Merle, after cautiously ascertaining the cost, invested in one between them, while Tattle, Nan, and Lizzie contented themselves with purchasing a few fishhooks and a ball of fine string.

"I suppose we ought really to take some bait with us," remarked Romola casually. "There isn't time, though, to go and dig for lob-worms. What's to be done about it?"

"Oh, we'll use limpets or anything else we can get," decreed Beata. "We'll find something along the rocks, you'll see. Mavis, where are we going? You know all the best walks. We elect you leader this afternoon."

"It's beautiful along the cliffs towards St Morval's Head. There's a path most of the way, and we can scramble where there isn't. I wouldn't have dared to take the children, but I vote we venture it."

"Anywhere you like so long as we don't waste any more time; I'm just crazy to start!" agreed Fay.

So they went by a narrow alley and up steep flights of steps to the hill above the town, and took the track that led along the edge of the cliffs towards St. Morval's Head. It was a glorious autumn afternoon, and, though the bracken was brown and withered, there were specimens of wild flowers to be picked and written down in the note-books. Summer seemed to have lingered, and had left poppies, honeysuckle, foxgloves, and other blossoms that were certainly out of season. Tattie, who was keen on entomology, recorded a red admiral, a clouded yellow butterfly, and a gamma moth, though she did not consider them worth chasing and catching for her collection.

Flocks of goldfinches and long-tailed tits were flitting about, and they spied some black-caps and pipits, and even a buzzard falcon poised in the air high above the cliffs. Here quite a little excitement occurred, for several sea-gulls attacked the buzzard and with loud cries tried to drive it away, following it as it soared higher and higher into the heavens, and finally routing it altogether and sending it off in the direction of Port Sennen.

Angela Brazil

The path along which the girls had been walking was the merest track through the bracken. So far there had been either a low wall or a hedge as a protection at the edge of the cliff, but now these outposts of civilisation vanished and they were at the very brink of the crags. Tattie, whose head was not of the strongest, turned giddy and refused to go farther; indeed, she was so overcome that she sank on the ground and buried her face in her hands.

"I daren't look down!" she shuddered. "I know I shall fall if I do. Oh! I wish I'd never come! How am I going to get back?"

"There's only about a hundred yards like this," urged Mavis. "After that the path is all right again. Take my arm."

"No, no! I daren't! I can't go either backwards or forwards. I feel as if I should faint!" sobbed Tattie, waxing quite hysterical.

Here was a dilemma! She must certainly be made to move one way or the other. With great difficulty Fay and Beata between them got her back to the path along which they had come, where she collapsed under the shelter of the wall, and sat down to recover.

"I'll be all right now," she said, wiping her eyes. "I can go home alone. Don't let me keep any of you."

"We'll come with you," said Lizzie Colville. "Nan and I don't like walking so near the edge either. I wouldn't cross that place for worlds."

So it was arranged that the Ramsays and the Castletons and Fay should go on to St. Morval's Head, while the rest of the company turned back.

"It's a pity, but it's no good taking people who turn giddy," commented Mavis. "If they can't manage that piece of cliff, how would they scramble down into the cove?"

"They haven't got tennis shoes on for one thing," remarked Merle, "and boots are horribly slippery. You ought to have rubber soles for these rocks. It just makes all the difference. Mavis and I always wear them at Chagmouth."

"So do we. We learnt that at Porthkeverne. We're used to scrambling. As for Fay she's a real fairy. I believe she could fly if you gave her a push over the edge to start her off."

"Don't try, thanks, or I might turn into a mermaid instead of a fairy or a bird! I often think, though, I'd like a private aeroplane of my own. They're things that are bound to come sooner or later. I only hope I shan't be too old to use one when they do. What a view it is here!"

The difficult piece of cliff had led them round a corner, and they were now facing a magnificent sweep of coast-line. Below them, fixed to a buoy that floated on the water, a bell was ringing incessantly, its clanging sound floating over the sea like the knell of a mermaid's funeral.

"It's to warn the vessels off the rocks," explained Mavis. "They can hear it in a fog when they can't see quite where they are." Merle and I always call it 'The Inchcape Bell.' Oh, you know the story?

> 'The worthy abbot of Aberbrothock
> Had fixed that bell on the Inchcape rock.
> On a buoy in the storm it floated and swung,
> And over the waves its warning rung.'

Then the pirate, Sir Ralph the Rover, goes and cuts it off, just out of spite, and sails away. Years afterwards his ship comes back to Scotland, and there's a thick fog, and he's wrecked on the very Inchcape rock from which he stole the warning bell.

> 'Sir Ralph the Rover tore his hair;
> He cursed himself in his wild despair.
> The waves poured in on every side,

Angela Brazil

And the vessel sank beneath the tide.'"

"Serve him right too! It was a sneaking rag to play!" commented Merle.

"The bell makes me think of an old hermitage," said Romola. "I expect to see a monk walking along, telling his beads. Who was St. Morval? Didn't he have a little chapel on the cliffs here?"

"Romola always thinks of the Middle Ages," laughed Beata. "That's because she poses so much for Dad's pictures. It sounds like a church bell under the sea to me. When we lived at Porthkeverne we were close to the lost land of Lyonesse, and there was a lovely story about a mermaid. They said she used to come and sit on a broad flat stone outside the church and listen to the singing; and the priest heard of it, so one day he came out and talked to her, and asked her if she wouldn't like to be baptized, and she said she'd think about it. So she swam away; but she came back again and again, and it was decided that she was to be baptized on Easter Sunday. But on Good Friday there was a terrible storm, and the waves came up and swallowed the whole of the village, so that when the poor mermaid arrived she found the church sunk under the sea, and the priest and all the people drowned. There was nobody to baptize her, and there never has been since, and she swims about the water weeping and singing any little bits of the service that she can remember. The fishermen said if anybody was at sea and heard her it was bad luck, and a sign he would certainly be drowned before long."

"I love the quaint old legends!" said Mavis. "I shall always think of your mermaid now, when I hear the bell. This is our way down to the cove. It's a most frightful scramble. Can you manage it?"

The girls went first over grass and gorse, then climbed down a tiny track so narrow and slippery they were obliged to sit and slide, and finally, with some difficulty, scrambled on to the grim rugged rocks beneath. They were on a kind of platform, covered with seaweed and little pools, and with deep swirling water below.

Beata decided it would be a good place to fish, so they got out their log-lines. The first and most manifest thing to do was to find bait. There were plenty of limpets on the rocks, and with penknives they managed to dislodge some of them. It was only when a limpet was caught napping that it was possible to secure him: once he sat down tight and excluded the air from his shell, no amount of pulling could move him. The victims thus gathered were sacrificed by Beata and Merle, who acted as high priestesses, and chopped them up, and placed them upon the hooks, for neither Mavis nor Romola would touch them, and even Fay was not particularly keen upon this part of the fishing operations. They were ready at last, and cast their lines. Merle, unfortunately, through lack of experience, had not unreeled hers far enough, and the heavy weight sank deeply in the water and jerked the whole thing out of her hands into the sea.

"Oh, what a shame! And we've only just paid two and sixpence for it! What an utter idiot I was! I never thought it would pull like that. See, it's floating about down there!"

"I'll get it for you if I can," said Beata. With some manoeuvring she managed to fling her own line over it and drag it slowly in, losing it several times but rescuing it in the end.

After that mishap Merle was wiser, and threw with more discretion. Fay also tried her luck, and the girls sat waiting for bites. But alas! none came. There were several false alarms, but the lines when hauled in held nothing more exciting than hunks of seaweed. It was really most disappointing.

"I'm afraid they don't like the bait," said Beata at last. "If we could find a few lob-worms now, it might tempt them. They're evidently rather dainty."

"And I expect we don't know much about it!" said Mavis.

"Well, people have to learn some time, I suppose. You can't tumble to fishing by instinct!"

It was decided to go farther along and try to find lob-worms. The difficulty was to scramble down the rocks on to the sand. From above it looked quite easy and possible, but at close quarters the crags were very precipitous. At one point, however, they determined to venture. They sat on the edge of the sloping rock, let go, and then simply slid down, hanging on to pieces of ivy and tufts of grass. The cove, when they thus reached it, was worth the trouble of getting there. Sand-gobies were darting about in the pools, and came swimming up to fight for the pieces of limpet which the girls dropped in for them. They found a few lobworms and re-baited their hooks and cast their lines afresh, but met with no better success than before.

"I'm fed up with fishing!" announced Romola at last. "Let's go home!"

She had voiced the general opinion of the party. All immediately began to wind up their lines.

"The tide's coming in fast, and we're close to the blow-hole," said Mavis. "It seems a pity not to stop and watch it."

The blow-hole was a curious natural phenomenon. The sea, pouring into a narrow gully, forced air and water to spurt through an opening at certain intervals. First a low groaning noise was heard, which waxed louder and louder until - so Beata declared - it resembled the snoring of Father Neptune. Then suddenly a shower of spray spurted from the aperture, the sunshine lighting it with all the prismatic colours of the rainbow. For a few seconds it played like a fountain, then died down as the wave receded. The girls were so interested in watching it that they quite forgot the sea behind them. While their backs were turned to it, the great strong tide was lapping and swelling in, moving higher and higher up the rocks, and covering the pools, and creeping into the cove, and changing the sand and seaweed into a lake. When Mavis happened to look round she found her basket floating. She started up with a cry. The one accessible spot where they had climbed down now had a deep pool under it.

"We must wade!" gasped Beata, and hurriedly pulling off her shoes and stockings she plunged as pioneer into the water.

She soon realised it was too dangerous a venture. The slimy seaweed underneath caused her to slip, and the strong swirl of the tide nearly swept her from her feet. With difficulty she splashed back again.

"We might swim it!" she suggested. "But what about our clothes?"

Mavis shook her head.

"We can't cross there till the tide goes down."

"Are we going to be drowned?" asked Romola, in a tremulous little voice.

"Certainly not!" - Mavis sounded quite calm and sensible - "we're safe enough here, but we're in a jolly nasty fix. We can sit above high-water mark, but it means staying till the tide goes down and that won't be for hours, and then it will be dark and how can we see to scramble up the cliffs?"

"I suppose we've got to wait till morning!" groaned Fay. "This is *some* adventure at any rate!"

"Rather more than most of us bargained for!" agreed Beata.

"I wouldn't care a nickel, only Mother'll be in such a state of mind when I don't turn up!"

Angela Brazil

"And Uncle David will be waiting to go home in the car. I wonder what he'll do?"

"They'll have the fright of their lives!"

"And we shall have the colds of ours!" shivered poor Romola. "October isn't exactly the month you'd choose for camping out. I wish we'd brought some more biscuits with us. I'm hungry!"

"Don't talk of biscuits or eating! I'm just ravenous."

Five very disconsolate girls found a sheltered corner under the cliff and squatted down to watch the sunset. There was a glorious effect of gold and orange and great purple clouds tipped with crimson, but they were none of them quite in the mood to appreciate the beauties of nature, and would much have preferred the sight of a tea-table. It was beginning to grow very cold. They buttoned their sports coats about their throats, and huddled close together for warmth. The sun sank into the sea like a great fiery ball, and the darkness crept on. Presently the moon rose, shining over the sea in a broad spreading pathway of silver, that looked like a gleaming fairy track across the water to the far horizon, where a distant lighthouse glinted at intervals like a fiery eye. The waiting seemed interminable. Romola, who felt the cold most, had a little private weep.

"I've always been crazy on stories of shipwrecks and desert islands," said Fay, "but when you go through it yourself somehow it seems to take the edge off the romance. I don't want any more to be a Robinson Crusoe girl! I'd rather stay warm with pussie by the fire."

"If we'd had a box of matches with us we might have lighted a fire!" sighed Beata. "Why *didn't* we bring some?"

"Why didn't we look at the tide and get home in decent time? It's no good crying over spilt milk!" grunted Merle rather crossly.

After that they all subsided into silence for a while. There was no sound except the monotonous lap of the waves. The sea-gulls and cormorants had flown past at sunset and gone to roost. The absolute quiet, and the dark shadows, and the silver light of the moon gave such an eerie atmosphere to the scene that presently Fay could stand it no longer.

"I guess I'll stir up the spooks!" she remarked, and scrambling to her feet she made a trumpet of her hands and called out a loud "Coo-o-ee."

To the immense astonishment of everybody an answering shout came from somewhere across the water. Instantly all sprang up and woke the echoes with their loudest possible lung-power. Before long came a splash of oars, and a boat, with a lantern fastened to its bow, entered the cove. It advanced cautiously to the rocks, and a tall boyish figure sprang out and held it steady, while some one in a fisherman's jersey stretched out a strong hand to help the girls to enter. Only when they were safely seated and the moonlight shone on their faces did Mavis recognise their rescuers.

"Mr. Penruddock - and surely not *Bevis*!" she exclaimed.

He enjoyed her amazement.

"I've got the week-end. There's been 'flu' at school, so they've sent some of us off while Matron fumigates the rooms. I thought I'd find you at the farm. There was a pretty to-do when it grew dark and you didn't turn up. The Doctor went to the Vicarage to ask if you were there, and they said you'd gone along the rocks fishing. So we took the boat and came to look for you. I say, you were in a jolly old mess, weren't you? Rather cold for sleeping out?"

"If we'd known you were coming over we wouldn't have started."

"I didn't know myself till the last minute. I'll bike over to

Angela Brazil

Durracombe to-morrow afternoon if I may? I haven't seen you and Merle for ages. You've given Chagmouth people an excitement! I should think half the town's waiting on the quay for you! We'd rather a business to find you. But 'all's well that ends well,' isn't it?"

CHAPTER VII

MUSICAL STARS

Mavis and Merle had not seen Bevis since last July, so they had an immense amount to talk about when he came over to Bridge House on the following afternoon. They had to tell him all their adventures during the summer holidays and about the changes at 'The Moorings,' and he also had much to relate about his own school and his future plans. Though he was now squire of Chagmouth, he took his new honours very quietly and made no fuss about them.

"It's something to feel I'm back at the old Coll. and can go on to Cambridge," he acknowledged in reply to the girls' questions. "The lawyers are very decent to me and give me pretty well all I want. In the spring I'm going to have a yacht of my own! They've promised me that. I'll take you both out for a sail in it."

"Oh, do! We shall just live for Easter!" rejoiced the girls.

"I wish it was holidays all the time!" added Merle. "What fun we'd have in your yacht!"

Such a wish, however, could certainly not be realised.

Bevis was due back at Shelton College, and 'The Moorings' claimed both Mavis and Merle. School might not be as exciting as yachting, but it had its interests. There was the

Magazine, of which Mavis was editress, and to which many spicy items were contributed; there was the Entertainments Club, which was getting up a piece to act at the end of the term.

In connection with this society, alack! a tremendous squabble ensued. It had fallen almost entirely into the hands of the boarders, and they seemed determined to keep all its privileges to themselves. They fixed upon a play, shared the cast among them, and held rehearsals in the evenings. Mavis, Merle, and Muriel, the only day-girls on the Committee, were furious.

"Where do we come in?" demanded Merle.

"It's too cool to settle everything without consulting us! We're as much on the Committee as you are! It's completely out of order!"

"Oh, what does it matter?" said Nesta, with aggravating easiness. "We can't bother to be always holding meetings. We wanted to set to work at once and rehearse, and there weren't enough parts to include day-girls. Can't you act audience for once? You seem very anxious to show off!"

"It's the pot calling the kettle black then, if we do!" retorted Muriel. "What about yourselves, I should like to know?"

The worst of it was that Miss Mitchell seemed to take the side of the boarders.

"I can't have you day-girls coming in the evenings to rehearse!" she decided. "No, I can't allow you to stay at four o'clock either, because the boarders must get their walk before tea. It would upset all our arrangements. Perhaps we may put some of you in a tableau, because that really wouldn't need much preparation."

A tableau! The day-girls felt much insulted! Miss Mitchell, who had seen them act in the history class, ought not thus to scout their talents. Merle took the matter particularly to heart because of her adoration for the new mistress. She was furiously jealous of the boarders, who could sit at meal-times at the same table as her idol, and could indulge in private chats with her during the evenings. Miss Mitchell was perfectly well aware of Merle's infatuation, but did not encourage it too deeply. She meant to be quite impartial, and to have no favourites. Moreover, she was very modern and unsentimental, and disliked what she called 'schoolgirl gush.' She had been the subject of violent admirations before, and knew how soon they were apt to cool down. She was perfectly nice to Merle, but a little off-hand, and never showed her any preference. This line of treatment rather aggravated Merle's symptoms instead of curbing the tendency.

"I'll *make* her like me!" she said to herself stubbornly.

The siege laid to the teacher's heart progressed slowly, partly because Merle's tactics were noticed by the others and became somewhat of a joke. Merle had placed a daily buttonhole of flowers upon the teacher's desk, but, led by Muriel, the Fifth form rallied, and one morning each of them appeared with a kindred posy and deposited her offering. Miss Mitchell turned quite pink at the sight of the eleven floral trophies. She was not absolutely sure how far it was meant for a 'rag.'

"This looks like a nature study competition!" she remarked. "I'm sure it's very kind of you all to bring me flowers, but unless it's my birthday or some special occasion I'm afraid I really don't know what to do with them. You can put them all in water at eleven, Nesta, but you mustn't waste time now fetching vases."

Merle, of course, never presented any flowers again. She brought a book to school one day that she had heard Miss Mitchell express a wish to look at, and, after lingering about in the classroom, plucked up courage to interrupt her idol, who was correcting exercises, and offer the loan of it.

The mistress, with her finger held to mark her place, looked up and shook her head.

"I've really no time for reading, thanks! At present my days are full from morning till night."

As direct means failed Merle turned to indirect. She wrote anonymous poems and popped them in the letter-box, hoping, however, that her writing might be recognised. Whether Miss Mitchell read them or not is uncertain; she made no mention at any rate of their receipt, and probably dropped them in the waste-paper basket. Merle would have been far more grieved over these repulses had there not been a counter interest at home. At the beginning of November Dr. and Mrs. Ramsay left the north altogether and came to settle at Durracombe. Naturally there were great changes at Bridge House. Jessop - the invaluable Jessop, who had been so many years in Dr. Tremayne's service - was leaving to take charge of a widower brother, and a young parlour-maid was coming in her place. Several rooms were cleared to make way for Dr. Ramsay's possessions, and a large motor van arrived bearing some of his furniture from Whinburn. Mrs. Ramsay was to have a little upstairs drawing-room of her own, in which to deposit her special treasures, and her husband was to turn the gun-room into his study. The delight and excitement of welcoming her father and mother made Merle temporarily dethrone Miss Mitchell in her heart. It was such fun to help to arrange all the things from home, and see how nice they looked in their new surroundings. Then Dr. Ramsay had brought his car, and of course Merle wanted to help to clean it and to go out with her father in it and coax him to allow her to drive. Everybody felt that it was ideal to have Mrs. Ramsay at Bridge House. She took the place of a daughter to Aunt Nellie, who was somewhat of an invalid, and would nurse her and manage the housekeeping for her instead of Jessop. She had always loved her native county of Devon, and rejoiced to return there instead of living in the north.

"I shall grow young again here!" she declared. "I'm going to try to find time to do some sketching. I've hardly touched my paintbox for years. Mavis and I must go out together and find subjects."

"While I drive Daddy about in the car!" decreed Merle. "I've told him I'm going to be his chauffeur as soon as I leave school. He didn't jump at the offer! Wasn't it ungrateful of him? He doesn't deserve to have a daughter! Oh, well, yes, I *did* run the car into the hedge yesterday, but there was no damage done, after all."

Dr. Tremayne thoroughly welcomed Dr. Ramsay as his partner. The calls of the practice had lately been growing too much for him, and he was glad tobe able to share the numerous visits, so the arrangement of joining households was a satisfaction to all concerned. Jessop wept when it came to the time of her departure.

"I've been here thirty-two years come Christmas!" she said. "I know it's the best for everybody, but I do feel it. I'm fond of my brother, and willing to look after him and the shop, but I'll miss the patients here! I've known many of them since they were born. At my age it's hard to make a change and settle down afresh."

"We'll motor over very often and see you, Jessop, and tell you all the news," consoled Mavis.

"I'll always be glad to welcome you and Miss Merle whenever you come. Let me know beforehand if you can, and I'll make you crumpets for your tea. You always like my crumpets!"

"Nobody else in the world knows how to make them properly," Merle assured her. "Those heavy things with holes in them that they sell in the shops simply aren't fit to be called by the same name!"

With Mother in the background to consult about matters of difficulty school seemed much easier, though not altogether without thorns. Last summer term Merle had considered herself the chosen chum of Iva Westwood, but now Iva had completely fallen into the arms of Kitty Trefyre. As they were both boarders and in the same dormitory, it was perhaps only natural they should be friends, yet it is never nice to be dropped, and Merle thought hard things of Iva. If she could have kept her feelings locked in her own breast it would not have mattered so much, but she was a true daughter of Jupiter, and, when provoked, could not refrain from shooting her arrows of bitter words. They quarrelled about the silliest trifles: the loan of an indiarubber, the loss of a pencil, or some slight differences of opinion, over which they would argue hotly. It was a pity, for at bottom Iva was a nice girl, and was merely passing through a phase from which she would probably soon have recovered if Merle would only have let her alone. On her side she might very well have contended that it is hard to be pinned to a single chum, and that she was perfectly at liberty to make fresh friends if she wished without of necessity giving offence to the old ones by so doing.

"Merle's so jealous!" she complained. "Why should she care? I'm sure I don't mind her walking about the school arm-in-arm with Beata Castleton!"

That, however, was exactly the point. Merle wanted Iva to mind, and was extremely annoyed because the incident left her unruffled.

One afternoon, in the musical appreciation class, the two had partly patched up past squabbles, and, for a wonder, were sitting side by side. The subject was 'Handel,' and for one of the illustrations Miss Mitchell called upon Merle to play the celebrated 'Largo.' She went through her performance quite creditably, took her music, and turned from the piano. Then she saw that during her absence Kitty had commandeered her seat next to Iva. For a moment Merle stood with a look of the blankest consternation, not knowing where to go, till Mavis beckoned and made a place for her, into which she thankfully slipped, squeezing her sister's hand surreptitiously, and feeling there was no friend in all the world so staunch as Mavis.

"If you wouldn't worry so over everybody, you'd get on better, dear!" advised the latter.

"I can't help caring! I wasn't born calm. It all matters so very much to me! What's the use of anything unless you care? You'd better swop me for a nice, little, tame, harmless sister guaranteed never to squabble even if people pull her hair, and always content to sit in the background everywhere!"

"She'd be very uninteresting!" laughed Mavis, bestowing a kiss upon Merle's apple cheek. "I think I prefer to keep you, thanks!"

"Thunderstorms and all?"

"So long as they clear the air, certainly! But we expect to have sunshine afterwards, please!"

Miss Mitchell intended to wind up her course of lessons on musical appreciation with a concert among the pupils, and certain of them had been bidden to play or sing. Naturally those on whom the choice fell went through agonies in the matter of practising. After hearing so much about great composers and the proper interpretation of their works, it seemed almost a liberty for schoolgirls to venture to give their rendering, and all felt that their performances would be subjected to decided criticism.

"It's the audience that will make me nervous!" fluttered Merle. "If I could play my piece when I'm alone and in the right mood and get a gramophone record taken of it that could be put on at the concert, I shouldn't mind. It would be rather fun sitting in a corner and listening to my own playing. Something like seeing my own ghost, wouldn't it?"

Mavis, Merle, Muriel, and Edith were all down for piano solos, Beata was to bring her violin, and Nesta, Iva, and Kitty were to sing. They would all do their best, but none had reached a very high level in the matter of attainment. Miss Mitchell, with memories of the splendid talent mustered at St. Cyprian's College in her own schooldays, felt that the concert would be a most modest affair.

"I wish we could get one or two good performers to come and help us!" she suggested.

"Durracombe isn't at all a musical place," admitted Miss Fanny. "There really isn't anybody whom we could ask. Mrs. Carey used to play, but she's out of practice and I'm sure she wouldn't venture before a roomful of schoolgirls."

"It would be rather an ordeal, I own."

About ten days before the event was to take place Muriel Burnitt had a tea-party at her own home to which she invited Miss Fanny, Miss Mitchell, and the elder boarders, asked them to bring their music, and went through all the programme of the little concert. It, in fact, answered the purpose of a dress rehearsal.

Mavis and Merle had not been included in the invitation and they were very much hurt.

"Muriel asked Beata, only she couldn't come. I know because Romola told me so. She even asked Babbie Williams!"

"It's most mean of her to miss us out!"

"When we're playing solos, too!"

The boarders talked tremendously about the pleasant evening they had had, and how very much they had enjoyed themselves.

"Muriel's aunt will be staying with her next week, and she's going to persuade her to sing at the concert!" said Iva. "She has a beautiful voice, and it will give things such a lift. Miss Mitchell is as pleased as Punch about it, and says that's just what we want. We ought to have one or two musical stars to make it go."

Muriel, who felt she had scored by securing a singer, took up a rather lofty attitude and made herself so objectionable that Merle raved in private, and even gentle Mavis was ruffled. They poured out their grievances at home.

"What's the date of the concert?" asked Mrs. Ramsay. "The 17th? Well, I have an idea! No! I don't mean to tell you now in case my scheme doesn't come off."

"What is it, Mummie? I'm curious."

"That's my secret! Take my advice and don't worry any more about Muriel. Things will probably turn out even in the end."

In spite of coaxing Mother refused to explain herself further, and it was only when a few days had gone by, and they had almost forgotten the incident, that one morning she opened a letter, read it, and clapped her hands in triumph.

"I've some lovely news for you! Cousin Sheila is coming to stay with us on the 16th, and she's actually bringing her friend Mildred Lancaster, the famous violinist! You know they both went to St. Cyprian's and were in the same form with Miss Mitchell. She'll be so pleased to meet them again! Cousin Sheila says Miss Lancaster promises to play at your school concert. Isn't that an honour? It will be something for you to tell Miss Mitchell, won't it? We'll ask her and Miss Fanny and some of the girls to tea while our visitors are here!"

This was indeed a delightful surprise. The name of Mildred Lancaster was one to conjure with in musical circles. She had just completed a most successful tour in Australia and America, and had won great applause. She was booked to give a recital in Exeter on the 15th, so that she would be in the neighbourhood and able easily to come on to Durracombe. She made her headquarters at Kirkton, so Mrs. Ramsay explained, but travelled much about the country playing at concerts. She was to be married in the spring to her old friend, Rodney Somerville, to whom she had been engaged for some years, but she did not intend to give up her music, and hoped still to make frequent public appearances.

"They're to have a flat in town," read Mother from Cousin Sheila's letter. "I'm so glad it's settled that way, because I want Mildred to be happy, yet it would be a wicked shame if she flung her talent to the winds, as some girls do when they marry. She'll have her own little home and yet go on with her career. I call it ideal!"

Mavis and Merle danced off to school simply brimming over with their news. It certainly had the desired effect. Miss Mitchell was very much thrilled at the prospect of meeting her old friends, and highly appreciated the privilege of a violin solo at the concert. The girls were, of course, most excited, except the performers, who nearly had hysterics at the prospect of playing before so great a musical star.

"I shall leave my violin at home!" wailed Beata.

"Nonsense! You'll find nobody more kind and encouraging than Miss Lancaster," said Miss Mitchell. "It isn't the great artists who find fault - they understand the difficulties only too well - it's the carping critics who can't perform themselves and yet think they know all about it! Do your best and no one will expect you to do any more!"

It was a great day for Mavis and Merle when their visitors arrived. They were fond of Cousin Sheila and welcomed her on her own account. With her companion they readily fell in love. Mildred Lancaster was a most charming personality, and although she had been so feted on concert platforms, she was absolutely simple and unaffected in private life. She had brought her wonderful Stradivarius violin, upon which she always played, and she took it out of its case and allowed the girls to admire its graceful curves, and its fine old varnish.

"It's my mascot!" she said. "I've had it all my life, and if anything were to happen to it I believe I'd give up music! It's been a great traveller, and always stays in my berth on sea voyages."

To say that the Ramsays were proud to escort Miss Lancaster and her Stradivarius to 'The Moorings' hardly describes their elation. A few parents and friends had been asked, so that with the school there was quite a large audience. It was arranged to take the girls' part of the programme first, and the visitors' solos afterwards, a proceeding for which the young performers were devoutly thankful. They got through their pieces very creditably, especially Beata, who won warm praise from Miss Lancaster.

"That child's artistic and will make a musician if she goes on with it. She puts *herself* into her playing."

"They're rather a remarkable family. Her sister is studying singing in London," purred Miss Pollard, pleased to have one of her pupils thus noticed.

The treat of the afternoon was when Mildred Lancaster began to play, and her entire mastery of her instrument was a revelation to most of the girls. They had never before had the opportunity of listening to such glorious music.

"The gramophone will sound like a ghost after this, however good the records!" declared Iva. "I wish I could hear her again."

"Miss Fanny's bringing fourteen of you to tea to-morrow - hasn't she told you yet?" exulted Merle.

Muriel had also been included in the invitation in spite of her previous discourtesy.

Angela Brazil

"It hurt *you* to be left out, so don't inflict the same feeling on anybody else!" urged Mrs. Ramsay when her younger daughter demurred. "Two blacks never make a white! The best way of 'getting even' with people is to do them a kindness. That stops the whole thing and sets it into a different groove. Ask Muriel if her aunt will come too. She sings beautifully, and perhaps she will bring her music."

The Ramsays' 'Musical At Home' was remembered for a long time by those girls who were present at it. Mother was a clever hostess, and she managed to put all her guests at ease and raise that magic atmosphere of enjoyment which only certain people seem able to create. The drawing-room looked charming with late flowers in its vases and a blazing log fire. Miss Mitchell, having snatched a private chat with her two old school friends, was radiant. Jessop, who had heard full details of the occasion, had insisted on coming over to bake the cakes, and hovered in the background like a beneficent deity, sending in fresh batches of hot crumpets. There were chocolates in little silver bonbonnieres and even crackers, though it was not yet Christmas. Aunt Nellie was there and enjoyed the music, and Dr. Tremayne and Dr. Ramsay joined them before the performance was over.

"Wasn't it a triumph? I think we know how to give a party!" rejoiced Merle in private afterwards.

"Yes, when Mother pulls the strings!" agreed Mavis.

CHAPTER VIII

YULE-TIDE

The end of the term was, to use Merle's expression, 'a little thin.' Miss Mitchell did not seem disposed to make any very great fuss about it, and merely set aside the last hour of the last afternoon for the play which the boarders had prepared. She suggested, indeed, that the day-girls might get up some tableaux, but as no one evinced any enthusiasm the matter dropped.

"Tableaux are rather tame unless you have most beautiful dresses," sniffed Muriel.

"It really isn't worth our while bothering over them," agreed Merle.

They were decidedly disappointed to have no chance to exhibit their own dramatic talents, but they were 'sporting' enough to give a hearty clap to the boarders' performance, a really magnanimous attitude on the part of Mavis, who had lent a pale pink silk dress to Nesta, and watched candle grease dropping down the front of it as that heroine pretended to investigate a smuggler's cellar with a light.

"Never mind! We'll have some acting of our own in the hols," she whispered to Merle, who sat next to her.

"Rather! And it will beat this simply into fits, though of course

Angela Brazil

I shan't tell them so."

The holidays this Christmas were to compensate for every disagreeable thing that had happened in the course of the term. First and foremost, and this ought to be written in big letters like a poster heading, BEVIS WAS COMING TO STAY. Mrs. Ramsay had invited him for a three weeks' visit to Bridge House, and he was to arrive on December 23rd. He had always been a great favourite with Dr. Tremayne, who thought that the boy's position was rather a lonely one, and that on this first Christmas in particular, after the solution of the mystery of his birth, he would feel the lack of any family of his own and would be glad to be welcomed by friends.

Naturally, to Mavis and Merle this was the event of greatest importance, but there was to be another pleasant happening as well. Cousin Clive was also coming to spend the holidays. He was Dr. Tremayne's grandson and his home was in London. The girls had never seen him, as he had not paid a visit to Durracombe during the last year, and they were very curious to know what he was like. Any misgivings which they may have cherished vanished instantly, however, at the first sight of Clive. He was a very big boy of twelve, as tall as Merle, with merry grey eyes that looked capable of fun. He was, of course, full of the affairs of his own preparatory school, but as he found they were ready to listen to his accounts of football matches or dormitory 'rags' he took them into his masculine confidence and extended the hand of friendship. He showed a particular fancy for Merle, whose robuster constitution allowed her to tear about with him and indulge in some rather hoydenish performances.

"You're a thorough tomboy!" said Mother, having called her younger daughter down from the coach-house roof, whither she had climbed in company with her cousin.

"Well, you see, Mummie dear, I have to amuse Clive!" was always Merle's excuse. "If I didn't keep him quiet he'd kick up no end of a racket and disturb Aunt Nellie. It's really very kind of me!"

"There's a large spice of enjoyment mixed with the philan-thropy!" twinkled Mother.

"Well, that's the right spirit. We ought to enjoy our own good deeds!" laughed Merle.

As Aunt Nellie was really a consideration in regard to noise, the young people had taken over the harness room as a temporary boudoir during the holidays. They carried down some basket chairs, tacked a few coloured pictures from annuals on its bare walls, and made it look quite pretty. Tom lighted them a blazing fire every day, and tended it during their absence with the care of a vestal virgin, so they were extremely cosy and jolly there. The joiner's bench and the glue-pot gave facilities for any hobbies they wished to carry on; they could make as much noise as they liked, and walk in and out with dirty boots, unreproved.

To Bevis this visit was elysium. All his experiences of young people had been confined to school, and he had never before spent such a holiday.

"It's grand to be in a home like this!" he said, once, to Mavis. "I can't help thinking, sometimes, how different life would have been to me if my mother had lived. It's hard not to have even the slightest remembrance of her. Suppose she had been here now and living at 'The Warren'!"

"You'll go there yourself some day."

"Perhaps. It'll be rather a forlorn business though, being in that big house with only a pack of servants. I believe I'll take a voyage round the world in a yacht. The fact is I can't quite see my future. I'm going to Cambridge, but after that things are vague. I always had dreams of a profession, but the lawyers say I ought to settle down on the estate. What's a fellow to do?"

"I wouldn't worry your head about it yet. There'll be plenty of time to think things over while you're at College," counselled Mavis. "Enjoy your holidays at any rate."

"No mistake about that. I'm having the luck of my life!"

It was only to Mavis's sympathetic ear that Bevis poured out these confidences. With Merle he was on different terms. He called her 'Soeurette' (little sister) and was always ready for some joke with her. She and Clive together led him a lively time, as well as keeping him busy helping them to make boxes, build a boat, and several other joinering enterprises.

"It does Bevis all the good in the world to be teased!" declared Merle.

"He certainly gets it, then!" laughed Mavis.

One special grievance had Merle. Bevis had devoted some of his spare time at Shelton College to taking motoring lessons, for he hoped to buy a car some day, and he could now drive so well that Dr. Ramsay trusted him at the steering-wheel.

"It's too bad!" declared that indignant damsel. "Just because Mother's nervous and thinks I'm going to run her into the ditch! Wait till I've had *my* course of motoring lessons! I'll take the shine out of Bevis! See if I don't!"

"You shall try my motor bike, if you like, Soeurette!" consoled Bevis. "That's to say, if they'll allow you."

"Don't, for goodness' sake, ask anybody, but just take it out on the quiet and I'll guarantee to ride it. Let's do it this very afternoon!" returned Merle, somewhat pacified.

On the whole the weather had proved exceedingly wet, so with the exceptions of a few runs in the car with the hood up, they had not ventured very far away, and had mostly taken walks in the neighbourhood. Bevis naturally wished to explore the

Durracombe district, and they had not been to Chagmouth since his arrival, and knew nothing of what was going on there. One drizzling morning, however, when they were all sitting in the harness room, they heard a clatter of hoofs and then a shout in the stable yard, and looking out of the window saw Tudor Williams on his little horse, Armorelle. The girls ran out at once.

"I say! How d'you do?" said Tudor. "Isn't your man about anywhere to take this horse?"

"Tom's in the greenhouse, I'll fetch him!" and Merle darted across the dripping yard.

"Have you come to see Uncle?" asked Mavis, stroking Armorelle's satin nose.

"No, I've a message from the Mater for you and Merle. Oh, here's your groom! Yes, just give her a wipe down, please" (as Tom led Armorelle away to the stable), "she's too fat and gets easily hot! Ugh! It's rather a horrid day. The Mater wanted to send me in the car, but I said I'd rather ride."

"Won't you come into the house?" asked Mavis.

"Or into our den?" invited Merle. "We've made the harness room into a snuggery."

"By Jove! Not a bad idea, that! Yes, take me there. I'm too splashed to be fit for the drawing-room. I say, this is no end! What a decent fire you've got!"

"You know Bevis? And this is our Cousin Clive," said Mavis, performing the introductions.

Tudor nodded, flung himself into a basket chair and looked round the room with some amusement.

"It's like you two!" he vouchsafed. "*I* should never have

Angela Brazil

thought of taking over the harness room! 'Pon my word, it's cosy! You won't want to turn out when I tell you what I've come for!"

"Turn out where?"

"Well, it's a long story. You see there are some new people come to live in Chagmouth - an artist with a family about a yard long. Of course, the Mater goes and calls and gushes and comes back talking about beauty and talent and all the rest of it. She's an eye to business though, has the Mater! Mr. Colville had asked her to get up a concert in aid of something or other, I don't know what it's for! The new Vicar's as bad as the old one for wanting money, and the Mater's perpetually raising the wind for the parish with entertainments. She's worked all her local stars rather hard, so you can imagine she pounced upon anybody new, and got them to promise about half the programme. She came back purring. There was the other half of the programme, though, to be fixed up. The Girl Guides had learnt a dialogue, so she said they might as well act it, and she had the posters printed and sent the school children round selling tickets."

"Well?" said Mavis, as Tudor paused for breath.

"I'm coming to the point fast enough! It seems the principal characters in the dialogue are three sisters, and yesterday one of them developed measles! The other two are contact cases and, of course, they're not allowed on the boards. You can't act 'Hamlet' without the Prince of Denmark and Ophelia and Polonius! It's the same business here. The dialogue has collapsed like a pricked balloon!"

"Have they no understudies?"

"Never heard of such things, and say it would take them six weeks to train any one else in the parts, besides which the others say they wouldn't dream of doing it without Gertie and Florrie or whatever their names are. The Mater sprinted round the village trying to fill up her empty programme but all her stars were huffy because they hadn't been asked before, and they said they had colds or they wanted to go to their grand-mothers' funerals, or some such excuse. Back comes the Mater almost in tears and says she really doesn't know whatever she's going to do about it, and there never was such a fiasco, etc. Then Babbie suggested 'Send for Mavis and Merle, they'll help you out.' Mother jumped to it like a drowning man at a rope. So I trotted off immediately after breakfast to ask if you'll come to the rescue."

"O-o-h! But when is the concert?"

"To-night at 7 prompt."

"Great Scott! We can't!"

"Yes, you can! Any of those impromptu things you give will simply delight people. They've paid their shillings and their sixpences to see some acting and they don't mind what it's like so long as it makes them laugh and they get their money's worth. The Mater'll send the car over for you after lunch and she'll put you up for the night - you, Talland, too, and you," nodding to Clive. "Be sporting, all of you, and come!"

"Could we possibly get through the thing we did last night?" hesitated Mavis, looking at the others.

"Let's try," decided Merle. "It's all gag, Tudor, and if we get stage fright and can't go on we shall just have to walk off, that's how it is."

"You won't do that! I say, you know, it's most awfully kind of you! The Mater will be *so* relieved. She'd have written a note but there was some other hitch about the refreshments and she was interviewing the schoolmaster. Shall we send the car at three? Then I'd better hurry home now and set the Mater's mind at rest."

"Wait, Tudor! We haven't asked Mother yet."

"Oh, didn't I tell you? I met Dr. and Mrs. Ramsay in your car and stopped them, and they both said 'Go, by all means.'"

"Well, we've let ourselves in for something!" exclaimed Mavis as Tudor rode away on Armorelle. "It was your fault, Merle!"

"No, it wasn't, it was yours! I think it will be rather fun! Cheer up, Bevis! Don't look such a scared owl! Here's old Clive absolutely peacocking at the idea."

"If I'm to be Isabella?" grinned Clive.

"Of course, if I'm Augustus!"

"Merle - you *can't!*"

"Who says I can't? The joke of it will be that nobody'll know. Clive and I are the same height and really rather alike, and if we change clothes they'll all think *he's* Augustus and *I'm* Isabella."

"Will anybody recognise me as Uncle Cashbags?" groaned Bevis.

"Not your nearest and dearest. Be as gruff as you can, and limp as you did last night. We're not going to let you off! Don't you think it! Why, we couldn't possibly do the piece without you!"

The young people, ostensibly for the entertainment of their elders, but largely for the amusement of themselves, had been acting in the evenings to an audience of Aunt Nellie, Uncle David, and Father and Mother. Their last performance had really been so successful that they felt they might venture to give it in so great an emergency. They began at once to pack their various properties.

"Rather a score to be asked to appear on a public platform! I wish Miss Mitchell could be there to see us!" triumphed Merle.

"The joke is that I don't believe Chagmouth people will recognise any of us," said Mavis, hunting for a pair of spectacles she had mislaid. "I'm going to bargain that our names aren't announced beforehand."

"Right-o! The audience can imagine we're a London Company on tour in the provinces, or anything else they like. They'll think far more of us if they don't know who we are till afterwards. Tudor mustn't give us away!"

CHAPTER IX

FACING THE FOOTLIGHTS

The big five-seater car came punctually at three and conveyed the young people and all their belongings to The Warren, where their arrival caused much satisfaction.

"You've saved us from a most awkward predicament," declared Mrs. Glyn Williams. "I hardly know how to thank you. Wasn't it clever of Babbie to think of it?"

"We've never forgotten how you did a scene here once!" said Tudor. "Couldn't do it myself to save my life! And Gwen says the same. Oh, here she is! I was looking for you, Gwen! Here are the Ramsays, and Talland."

The Gwen who advanced to shake hands was so different from their old acquaintance that the girls felt they scarcely would have recognised her. She did her hair in a new fashion, and was wonderfully grown-up, and even more patronising than formerly. She said a languid "How d'you do," then left Babbie to entertain them, which the latter did with enthusiasm, for she was fond of Mavis and Merle.

"I expect you're thinking of all the improvements you'll make here when you come of age?" said Mrs. Glyn Williams, trying to be pleasant to Bevis over the tea-cups. "It's a nice place, and will really look very well when it's been redecorated. You'll have to do it up for your bride, won't you?"

At which joke Bevis blushed crimson and dropped his cake on the carpet, to his own confusion and the delight of the fox-terrier Jim, who thought it was done for his especial benefit, and promptly swallowed the piece, icing and all.

"I don't want to hurry you to turn out," protested Bevis shyly.

"Oh, we shall have Bodoran Hall ready by that time. We were there last week looking at the new building. The workmen are really beginning to get on with it at last."

"You'll have to build fresh stables here, Talland, if you mean to do any decent hunting," advised Tudor airily. "If I were you I'd get those lawyers to start them at once, then they'd be ready when you want them. I suppose you *will* hunt?"

"I'm not sure yet what I mean to do," replied Bevis guardedly.

He did not like so much catechism about his future plans. In the old days of his poverty he had never admired the Glyn Williams' ideals of life, and he had no wish to mould himself upon their standards. The sporting landlord, with a horizon bounded by the local meet or a county ball, was a type that did not appeal to him, and he saw no reason why he should be forced by a spurious public opinion into lines that were uncongenial. Though on the surface he and Tudor were friends, at bottom the old antagonism existed as in the days when they had quarrelled on the cliffs near Blackthorn Bower.

It was only to please Mavis and Merle that he had accepted this invitation to The Warren, where he found himself in the peculiar position of being patronised in his own house.

With Bevis rather gloomy and restrained, Tudor slightly aggressive, and Gwen too fashionable to trouble to entertain her old friends, matters were not as exhilarating as they might have been, and everybody seemed relieved when it was time to walk down to the Institute.

"I suppose I shall have to go!" yawned Gwen. "These village concerts of Mother's are *such* a nuisance! Why can't the people get up their own instead of always expecting her to bother with them! *I* don't want to hear Miss Smith and Miss Brown and Miss Robinson! It bores me stiff."

"Not very polite of her when *we* are going to act!" whispered Merle to Mavis as they put on their hats.

"It certainly isn't! But Gwen's always like this. I vote we try not to mind," returned Mavis heroically.

The entertainment was to be given in the local Institute, which was fitted with a platform and curtain, but otherwise held no great facilities for theatricals. A large and very unruly crowd of young people were outside waiting for admission, and through these our party had to push their way to a side entrance. At the back of the platform great confusion raged. The whole of the Castleton family seemed to be trying to dress one another among a rich jumble of costumes, while Mr. Castleton, altering the poses in his tableaux at the eleventh hour, kept sending messengers home to his studio for articles which he had forgotten.

"The pantry's the only place for the Ladies' Dressing-Room, and it's full of tea-cups!" said Beata, kneeling on the floor to button Lilith into a mediaeval robe that reached to her toes.

"Tea-cups or no tea-cups, I'll have to use it!" said Merle. "Come with us, Romola, and mount guard over the door while we change. I'm not going to have all the parish popping in. How sublime you look!"

"Very hot and uncomfortable!" sighed Romola. "I'd put on the blue costume and then Dad suddenly altered the whole tableau and made me get into this instead. Wasn't it tiresome of him? Now he's fussing about and I know we shall be late! We always are!"

"So shall we be if we don't hurry up. Have you got the right bag, Mavis? Oh, here are some of Bevis's things! I must rush out and give them to him before we begin."

Dressing in a pantry full of tea-cups, by the aid of candles and a hand-mirror, was not at all an easy performance, but the girls did their best for one another and were pleased with the result. As soon as they were ready they went to help Bevis and Clive, who needed much assistance, and were beginning to suffer from stage-fright.

"I was a silly owl to let myself in for it!" groaned the former. "I expect I'll forget every word I ought to say and disgrace myself!"

"You'll do nothing of the sort!" declared Merle firmly. "If you could act it last night you can act it to-night, so don't be ridiculous. You've just *got* to - there!"

"All right, Soeurette! Don't get baity! I won't let you down if I can help it!"

The audience by this time had been admitted, and had surged into the room and struggled for seats, slightly restrained by the boy scouts, who were acting as stewards, and who vigorously turned out the rank and file if they invaded the reserved benches. The noise was tremendous, everybody was talking, and rough lads at the back were indulging in whistling and an occasional cat-call.

"The tickets have gone well, at any rate," said Nan Colville, who was helping in one of the tableaux. "It's something to have the room full, Dad says! But just listen to them! Aren't they rowdy?"

"If everybody's ready we really *must* begin!" declared the Vicar, making a hurried visit behind the scenes. "I don't think they'll wait any longer."

Furious stamping from the audience endorsed his words, so Mr. Castleton, who had contemplated yet another alteration, was obliged to be content and allow the curtain to go up. The scene was 'the first meeting of Dante and Beatrice,' and was a charming presentment of mediaeval Italy. Constable, robed in pale green velvet with a Florentine cap on his picturesque curls, made a very glorified representation of the youthful poet, while Lilith, in the traditional red dress described in the *Vita Nuova*, looked ethereal enough to inspire a lifelong devotion and whole volumes of poems.

The rest of the Castleton family, and a few friends, were grouped as relations and nobles, in some of the richest dresses of the studio, and made a very brave show, evoking much applause. It was years since the villagers had seen 'Living Pictures,' and this was superior to anything of the sort given before. Without the Castletons the entertainment would have been almost non-existent. They provided the greater half of the programme. They were so accustomed to posing as models that they took most graceful positions in the tableaux, and preserved their postures admirably without moving so much as a finger. They included Babbie in a scene from *The Vicar of Wakefield*, and she made a dear little 'Sophia' in muslin dress and mob cap, hugely to her mother's satisfaction.

Morland, who was at home for Christmas, gave two piano solos, and though his beautiful artistic playing was much above the heads of most of the audience, there were some who were musical enough to enjoy it. Everybody appreciated Claudia's songs. Her voice was of a rare quality, and even the rough lads at the back of the room stopped 'ragging' and listened in silence. It was very highly trained singing, but held that divine throb of passion which uses art as the instrument of nature, and united the correctness of a musician with the spontaneous carolling of a bird. With youth and so pretty a face added to her talent it was no wonder that Claudia had an ovation.

"I'm not supposed to sing anywhere in public till I've finished with the college," she announced behind the scenes. "Signor

Arezzo would be simply furious if he knew. He's a terrible Turk about it. I don't see how he's going to get to hear about it though! I shan't tell him myself, you may be sure."

Fay, who had considerable skill at elocution, gave a most amusing recitation, to which Morland played a very soft and subdued accompaniment on the piano, and for the encore that followed she repeated some quaint poems of American child-life, which were such a success that the Vicar mentally voted her a discovery, and decided to ask her to help the programme on future occasions.

It was now the turn of our party from Durracombe, who were trying to keep up one another's spirits behind the scenes. The audience, owing to long sitting still, was growing a little obstreperous. The chairman had to keep constantly ringing a bell and reminding people to be quiet. The noise at the back waxed so violent that his voice could hardly be heard, and the occupants of the front seats had to turn round and shout, 'Order!' 'You'll be turned out!' before the delinquents preserved a decent hush. The little piece evolved by Mavis and Merle was entitled:

A Rich Relation.

The first scene disclosed Mrs. Hardup, a widow lady, lamenting her lack of means, and regretting that her son, Augustus, should have engaged himself to Isabella, a charming but utterly impecunious damsel. She cheered up, however, when the young people came in bearing a letter; for it was from Uncle Cashbags, their rich relation, announcing that he was coming that very day to have lunch with them. Mavis, as the diplomatic widow, with grey hair and tortoise-shell-rimmed spectacles, looked at least fifty, and preserved her disguise admirably. As for Merle, not a soul in the audience would have recognised her as Augustus. She wore Clive's Eton suit and overcoat, had a brown wig and a moustache, and affected a deep-toned fashionable drawl. Clive, arrayed in some of Mrs. Ramsay's garments, with a hat and veil and a fur,

Angela Brazil

looked a thorough member of the smart set and acted the most modern of modern damsels. He entered, affectionately leaning on the arm of Augustus, and almost embarrassed that youth by his attentions.

Bevis, as Uncle Cashbags, with white hair, long beard, false eyebrows, and a gouty foot, came limping on to the stage, and was received with effusion by the widow and Augustus, and especially by Isabella, who was a minx, and set herself to captivate the old gentleman. In vain the luckless Augustus tried to ingratiate himself with his rich relation; he was unfortunate enough to tumble over the gouty leg and make several other most exasperating mistakes, which ended in Uncle Cashbags wrathfully repudiating him as his heir, and announcing his intention of marrying Isabella himself, finally hobbling away with the fair and faithless damsel clinging fondly to his arm and blowing a good-bye kiss to her former fiance.

Mischievous Clive was in his element, and played the part with such tremendous zeal that the audience, who had not yet grasped his youth and his sex, watched his manoeuvres breathlessly, and several old ladies looked quite scandalised and disapproving. It was only when called before the curtain that, at a whisper from Mavis, he pulled off hat and veil, revealing his unmistakably boyish head, whereupon a great shout of laughter arose from the benches and a perfect storm of applause.

"It has been capital! Capital!" said Mrs. Glyn Williams. "One of the best entertainments we've ever had at the Institute! Didn't Babbie look sweet as 'Sophia'? We must have some more tableaux another time. Gwen, you ought to have been in too! The Castletons were splendid! Such a number of nice young people here! We ought to have a little dance. They must all come up to The Warren to-morrow evening, and we'll clear the drawing-room. I'll telephone to Dr. Tremayne and say I'm keeping you four till Friday. Your dresses? Oh, we'll send over for them. I'm sure your Mother won't mind your staying!"

There was no possibility of refusal, for Mrs. Glyn Williams had quite settled the matter, and invited the Castletons and the Macleods and the Colvilles and several other people on the spot. The Ramsays, who had made plans of their own for the following evening, felt a little caught, especially as Bevis looked glum and reproachful.

"How *could* you?" he said to Mavis in an agonized whisper.

"How could I help it?"

"We were shot sitting," murmured Merle. "Cheer up, Bevis! A dance is a dance, anyway. I hope I haven't spoilt Clive's Etons for him!"

Mrs. Glyn Williams really meant to be very kind and to give the young people pleasure, and if Bevis did not entirely appreciate her hospitality it was no doubt his own fault. The fact was that the snubs which he had received as Bevis Hunter still rankled, and though as Bevis Talland he was on a very different footing, he found it difficult entirely to forget all that had gone before.

"I was exactly the same as I am now, but no one would notice me till I came into the estate - except you and Merle!" he said once rather bitterly to Mavis. "I sometimes feel their friendship is hardly worth having!"

"It's the way of the world, and you have to take people just as they are," she replied. "It's no use keeping up ill-feeling, Bevis. If they hold out the olive branch, it's more gracious to accept it, isn't it?"

"Oh, I'll behave myself! But all the same, I discriminate between my old friends and my new acquaintances; I'd rather not call them by the name of friends!"

There were great preparations next day at The Warren. The furniture was carried out of the drawing-room, the parquet

Angela Brazil

floor was polished, and Chinese lanterns were hung up in the conservatory, and the cook was busy preparing light refreshments. It was a pretty house for a dance, and looked very gay and festive with its Christmas decorations of holly and ivy, and its blazing fire of logs in the hall. Mavis's and Merle's party dresses duly arrived, and they made careful toilets, coming downstairs shyly, to feel a little in the shade by the side of Gwen the magnificent, who, alack! was trying to copy the up-to-date manners of some of her new school friends, with rather unhappy results. Perhaps kind little Babbie noticed the Ramsays' embarrassment, for she went to them at once to give them their programmes.

"How nice you look!" she said. "Isn't it always a horrid time, just when every one is arriving? It's ever so much nicer when the first dance has started!"

There were a great many people present whom Mavis and Merle did not know. Some of these were introduced by Tudor, and asked for dances, and very soon the sisters were separated and gliding over the polished floor with partners.

Mrs. Glyn Williams, having welcomed the young guests, retired to a sofa for a chat with some other dowagers, and left them to fill up their programmes as they liked. There were far more ladies present than gentlemen, so it was a case of girls dancing with one another. Merle readily whisked away with Tattie, or Nan, or Lizzie, but shy Mavis, after the first two-step, stood in a corner unnoticed. Gwen was enjoying herself very much with the pick of the partners, Beata and Romola floated by together, and Clive was carefully performing his steps in company with a much amused married lady. Mavis acted wallflower for several dances, feeling considerably out of it, till Bevis's voice sounded suddenly in her ear.

"Why, here you are! I've been looking for you everywhere! How many dances can you give me? I've kept my programme as free as I could till I found you. I thought the pixies must have spirited you away! What did you say? I ought to ask

Gwen? It isn't necessary in the least. You know I'm a duffer at it, and I should probably tread on her toes and she'd hate me for evermore. May I have these four?"

"Give half to Merle!"

"Soeurette's perfectly happy with the kids! If you won't let me have them I won't dance at all. I'll hide in the conservatory, or run away into the garden. You promised to be my teacher!"

"So I will, but I feel I mustn't monopolise you. Oh, dear! Well, if you've written them down I suppose it will have to be!"

"May I have the pleasure, Miss Ramsay?" twinkled Bevis, offering his arm.

"Thanks very much! You may!" laughed Mavis.

"I'm always glad when I get my own way!" chuckled Bevis, as they started a valse.

Three of the dances which Bevis had appropriated on Mavis's programme came in succession, and as their steps went well together they thoroughly enjoyed themselves. At the close of the third they were walking into the hall to get lemonade when Mrs. Glyn Williams smilingly stopped them.

"I want to introduce you to some fresh partners. There are plenty of people anxious to know you!" she said to Bevis archly. Then, tapping Mavis with her fan, she continued, laughing, "Naughty girl! You mustn't keep him *all* to yourself! I really *can't!* allow it!"

Poor Mavis blushed magenta, and stood aside while her hostess whisked the unwilling Bevis away and remorselessly fixed up the rest of his programme for him. She did not attempt to find a partner for Mavis, who was too overwhelmed with confusion to care to dance even with Lizzie Colville, and who backed towards the piano and began to turn over the music. Inwardly

Mavis was raging, though she had sufficient pride to preserve an outward calm.

"If there's anything here you know I'd be grateful if you could play it and give me a rest, my hands are so stiff," said Mrs. Colville, who had volunteered to act as pianist for the evening.

"I'll try with pleasure!" answered Mavis, taking her place.

She was glad to have an excuse for not dancing. She only wished she could have run away from The Warren and gone straight home and poured out her troubles to her mother. The Glyn Williams had cut Bevis in the old days and poured scorn on the Ramsays for knowing him, and it seemed too bad that their present hospitality to him should still be a subject for blame. Mavis's pride kept her at the piano all the rest of the evening. She was a good reader, and assured Mrs. Colville that she liked playing. She shook her head when Bevis came for his fourth dance.

"*Please* get another partner! I'm busy here! Mrs. Glyn Williams will find you somebody!"

Whereupon Bevis, muttering very uncomplimentary remarks about his hostess under his breath, deliberately passed by several eligible wallflowers, chose out the youngest child in the room, and led her off in a valse.

Merle, who was still an absolute schoolgirl and revelled in anything in the nature of a party, enjoyed her evening supremely. Mavis was very glad when it was all over and she was quiet in bed. Some new element seemed to have entered to-night into her old happy world and to have rubbed the bloom off her innocent friendship with Bevis.

"It was so jolly in the old days when we hunted for primroses and had picnics in Blackthorn Bower!" she thought. "It's not ourselves who have changed, but other people who won't allow us to be the same. Why couldn't things go on as they were? If this is society I don't like it! Oh, dear! I wish we could always stay exactly as we are and never grow up at all!"

CHAPTER X

THE MUMPS

When the Christmas holidays were over, a very important decision was arrived at with regard to Clive. For many reasons his parents considered his preparatory school too strenuous for him, and, as he had considerably outgrown his strength, it was arranged to allow him to miss the spring term and to stay at Durracombe until Easter. He was to go every morning to the Vicarage for private lessons from Mr. Carey, and he was to be out of doors as much as possible, drink plenty of milk, and try, as his grandfather expressed it, to 'put on flesh.' Master Clive himself was only too well content to have what he justly considered a continuation of his holidays. He did not mean to be too clever over his lessons at the Vicarage, and, indeed, he planned to make a little work go a long way. Being out of doors as much as possible suited him exactly. He strutted about Durracombe, with a rolling naval walk, making friends with everybody, and telling them he had quite determined to go to sea and become an Admiral. He went out motoring with his grandfather or Dr. Ramsay, and he spent a considerable portion of time with Tom, the old gardener, who was long-suffering in many ways, though roused to wrath by any injury to his young bedding-out plants. Mrs. Ramsay 'mothered' Clive, feeling it was some return for the kindness which Uncle David had shown to her own girls. She grew fond of the young scapegrace and covered his escapades as far as possible, so as not to alarm nervous Aunt Nellie, who would have been much perturbed at some of her grandson's reckless performances.

There was no harm about Clive; he was simply a young, restless, fast-growing boy, who constantly wanted fresh outlets for his energies. He loved to tease his cousins, but met his match in Merle, who generally turned the tables and carried the war into the enemy's camp. When they were not sparring or playing jokes upon one another, the two were firm allies. Merle had always wished for a brother, and lively Clive was a companion after her own heart. Mrs. Ramsay, indeed, complained that her younger daughter was becoming an utter tomboy, but she was glad for the two to be together, as she could trust Merle not to allow her cousin to go too far, and to keep him from endangering either his own limbs or the safety and comfort of other people.

The Spring term had advanced only a few weeks when a most untoward thing happened. Merle got mumps! How she picked them up nobody knew, but, as mother said, in a doctor's house you may always be prepared to catch anything, and it was a marvel the children had had so few complaints. Merle was not really very ill, but her face and neck were swollen and painful, and, worst of all, she was considered in a highly infectious condition and was carefully isolated in a top bedroom. Neither Mavis nor Clive had had mumps, and it was hoped they might escape, though as they had been with Merle the germs might still be incubating. Mavis was, of course, not allowed to go to 'The Moorings,' and Clive was debarred from his lessons at The Vicarage, and they had to preserve a species of quarantine, equally trying to them both, for at Dr. Tremayne's suggestion Mavis turned temporary governess to Clive and coached him in several subjects in which he was deficient. The young rascal, highly aggrieved at this unexpected tuition, took liberties with his gentle cousin which he would not have dared to take with Mr. Carey, and extracted as much fun as possible from his studies. Mavis was quite sure he made mistakes on purpose, and pretended to be stupid in order to reduce the standard of what was required, but the main object was to keep him quiet and out of mischief, and her teaching served that end at any rate.

Angela Brazil

"I wouldn't be a mistress in a boys' preparatory school if they offered me a thousand a year!" she told Mother. "I'd rather clean doorsteps, or sew buttons on shirts at a farthing a dozen, or sell watercress, or wash dishes in a restaurant!"

"Nonsense! It's not so bad as all that, surely!" laughed Mrs. Ramsay. "If you knew how the little wretch rags me! I only wish it was Merle who had to teach him and that I had the mumps instead. It must be nice and quite comfortable by the fire upstairs!"

Merle, however, did not at all appreciate the privilege of being ill and confined to one room. She was not so fond of indoor amusements as her sister, and soon tired of reading and drawing and games of patience. Her great grievance was that she was left so much alone. Mrs. Ramsay had to attend to Aunt Nellie, to answer the telephone, and to interview patients who came while the doctors were out and to take their messages, as well as to do the housekeeping, so she was kept constantly busy and had not much time to sit upstairs with Merle. Dr. Tremayne and her father paid her flying visits, but these were too short to content her.

"What's five minutes out of a long day?" she asked. "It's too bad! When Mavis used to have bronchitis we all almost lived in her bedroom. Nobody makes the least fuss about *me*! You don't even look decently sorry or very sympathetic! You come smiling in as if mumps were a sort of joke. It isn't a smiling matter to me, I can tell you. I'm fed up with them!"

"Poor old lady! It's a shame to laugh at your big face! Shall I cry instead?" said Father.

"It wouldn't seem quite so heartless!" retorted his indignant patient.

Next day Merle received a letter, which was pushed under the door. It was all in rhyme, and as it was in Dr. Ramsay's handwriting she concluded that her father must have sat up late the night before courting the muse of poetry. His verses ran as follows:

MERLE WITH MUMPS

When Merle was suffering from the mumps
She felt most down and in the dumps;
Her friends, to cheer her up the while,
Laughed at her face to make her smile.

But eyeing with reproach her folk
She told them 'twas a sorry joke.
"Hard-hearted wretches," so she cried,
"To jeer while here upstairs I bide!"

Having no bad intent to tease her,
But wishing only just to please her,
Her family then ceased their jeers
And showed their sympathy in tears.

Her mother, who her pillow set,
Dropped tears and made the room quite wet,
And gurgled forth, "Alack-a-day,
That here upstairs with mumps you stay!"

Her uncle just outside the door
Sobbed till his chest was hoarse and sore,
And, swallowing in his throat some lumps,
He mourned, "My Niece has got the mumps"

The maids who came her plight to see
Splashed tears in cups of milk or tea;
The room it grew so very damp
Her limbs began to feel the cramp.

Her father to her chamber crept,
And lifted up his voice and wept;
With kerchief of capacious size
He stood and groaned and mopped his eyes.

Angela Brazil

So big the tears that from him fell
They were enough to make a well,
And, standing in a pool of water,
He sighed, "Alack! my mumpsy daughter!"

"Stop! Stop!" cried Merle, "O don't be sad!
These waterworks will drive me mad!
Good gracious, how I wish you'd smile
Instead of weeping all the while!

"Cheer up, for goodness' sake, I pray,
And treat me in your usual way.
No more I'll call you hearts of leather,
In spite of mumps we'll laugh together!"

Perhaps the family thought they had not done enough to
relieve the tedium of Merle's banishment; at any rate they set
to work and made great efforts to amuse her. Mavis sketched
her portrait, adding wings and a halo, and printed underneath
"Saint Merle suffering her Martyrdom." Mother clicked away
on the typewriter, and deposited a document in her daughter's
room, which claimed to be:

Extract from "The Durracombe and Devon Times"

SOCIETY GOSSIP

It is with sincere regret that we record the indisposition of that
leader of our local social life, Miss Merle Ramsay. Well known
for her dramatic talent, she lately acted the part of principal
boy at an important performance held in Chagmouth, the
Metropolis of the West. Her audience, which included some of
the most celebrated critics and press representatives of the
neighbourhood, was unanimous in acknowledging her spirited
conception of what was certainly a difficult and delicate role,
which, in less skilled hands than hers, might have degenerated
into buffoonery or sheer melodrama. She was greatly to be
congratulated on her achievement, and it is hoped this is not
the last time she will appear on the boards and give Devon

audiences the opportunity of enjoying her rare humour. It may be noted that, in addition to her powers of dramatic representation, Miss Ramsay has no mean record in the world of sport.

Her athletic proclivities are marked, and she has the distinguished honour of being president of the Games Club at that great west country centre of education 'The Moorings.' Among her many activities Miss Ramsay numbers a facility in music and an affection for horticulture; she has travelled much in the immediate neighbourhood of Durracombe, and her favourite hobby is motoring.

Miss Ramsay, who through the nature of her indisposition was unable to afford our press representative a personal interview, sent messages of thanks for the local sympathy expressed for her condition.

"It is a matter of much gratification to me to know that I am missed," were her words; "I trust soon to be back at work and to be able to fulfil my many engagements." At the request of the local Entertainments Committee we are asked to state that, owing to the absence of their most prominent member, no further performances will be given for the present. We wish Miss Ramsay a speedy return to health.

Merle laughed very much over these literary effusions, and they certainly had the effect of cheering her up. What she pined for chiefly, however, was company. She had a very sociable disposition and hated to be alone. She particularly missed Clive, who had grown to be her best playfellow. She begged for the dog or the cat to share her solitude, but that was strictly forbidden on the ground that they might be germ-carriers and convey the mumps to others. One day she was sitting at her table trying to amuse herself with an everlasting game of patience, when she suddenly heard peculiar noises on the roof above. There was a scraping and bumping, as if an eagle or some other enormous bird had alighted there. The sounds continued till at last there was a thump on the skylight and Clive's mischievous face appeared grinning down at her.

Immensely thrilled she lifted the window, and he crawled farther along and thrust his head through.

"Hello, old girl! How are you getting on? I say! You do look rather a sight! I wanted to have a squint at you! Are you going to have your photo taken?"

"Don't be a young beast! How did you get up here?"

"They're repainting the house next door, so I took French leave and borrowed the tall ladder. I've had rather a business clambering about till I found your window. I say, does your face hurt?"

"Not much now, but it did at first."

"You look like the picture of the fat woman at a fair!"

"Wait till you get it yourself, and then I'll jeer."

"I'm awfully sorry for you! Look here, I've brought you some toffee. Can you catch it if I throw it down? I've finished that boat we were making. Tom helped me. Mavis is hemming some sails; then I'm going to try it on the reservoir. I wish you could come with me!"

"So do I," said the patient dolefully. "But that's out of the question. Don't you think you ought to be going back? Suppose somebody takes away the ladder!"

"I'd drop down into your room then."

"And catch the mumps?"

"Shouldn't much care if it meant missing my lessons!"

"I can hear somebody coming upstairs!"

"I'll be off then. Ta-ta! You're not exactly beautiful, but on the whole you don't look so bad as I expected. You needn't tell anybody I came! Bye-bye!"

On the 14th of February Merle was still a prisoner. She had almost forgotten there was such a saint as St. Valentine, so it came as a great surprise to find certain mysterious parcels brought up on her breakfast tray. There were flowers and a packet of chocolates, and a new game of solitaire, and an amusing little mascot dog with a movable head. It was almost like having a birthday. On the top of the parcels was an envelope addressed in a disguised handwriting. It contained a sheet of pink paper bearing the picture of a heart pierced by an arrow, while Cupid drew his bow in the distance. Underneath was written:

"Sweet Merle, of Durracombe the belle,
Accept this heart that loves you well:
A heart most tender, kind, and true,
That lives and beats for only you!
'Twere cruel in this faithful heart
To plant and fix so big a dart,
So heal its wound I beg and pray,
And be my VALENTINE to-day!"

The sender, as is usual in valentines, remained anonymous, and Merle could only guess at the authorship, though she had strong suspicions of Daddy and taxed him with it.

"St. Valentine never lets out secrets!" he twinkled. "He's a most discreet old gentleman. People don't make as much use of him as formerly. Very foolish of them, for he came in extremely handy. It's a pity to let good old customs drop. A St. Valentine revival society might be rather a good idea. By the by, that heart isn't anatomically correct! It looks more like a specimen from a butcher's shop than the human variety!"

"Don't be horrid!" laughed Merle. "You can't expect Cupid to know the difference! He's sent me some nice things. Aren't there any more saints in the calendar who bring presents?

Angela Brazil

What's the next red-letter day?"

"Nothing till Shrove Tuesday, my dear, and by that time, I hope, you'll be downstairs again, and eating your pancakes with the rest of the family."

CHAPTER XI

BAMBERTON FERRY

Miss Pollard was extremely nervous on the subject of the mumps. She insisted upon waiting until long after the usual period of disinfection before she would allow Mavis and Merle to return to 'The Moorings.'

"One can't be too careful!" she fluttered. "I know in a doctor's house they are apt sometimes to take these things too lightly. It's far better not to run any risks."

As Merle had a medical certificate of complete recovery, and neither Mavis nor Clive had developed the complaint, there was now no reason for keeping the girls away from school, and one Monday morning they were received back into the fold. They had lost a considerable amount of ground in regard to their lessons, and had to work hard to try to make up for the weeks that were missed. At hockey, too, Merle found her teams were slack. It needed much urging to persuade them to play a really sporting game.

"I daren't fix a match yet with any other school," she assured them. "We should only be beaten hollow, and it's no use playing if we have no chance to win. You must all buck up and get more into the swing of things. Perhaps next season we shall be a stronger team."

"If we never play matches we shall never improve," objected

Sybil, who was anxious to accept the challenge of the Beverton County School.

"We've got the credit of 'The Moorings' to think about!" snapped Merle. "You wouldn't like them to go home crowing they'd absolutely wiped us off the face of the earth? I've had a little experience in matches and I know what I'm talking about. It would be downright silly to give ourselves away."

Sybil was rather a thorn in Merle's side. She had come from another boarding-school, and on the strength of this experience thought she hadthe right to become at once a leader at 'The Moorings.' She was very disgusted not to be in any position of authority, and consoled herself by continual criticism of the monitresses, particularly Merle, with whom she was always sparring. She was a curious character, all precept but not much practice. She loved to give good advice and to lay down the law, and was rather priggish in bringing out moral maxims for the benefit of others. She had a tremendous sense of her own importance and what was due to her, and was very ready to consider herself overlooked, or neglected, or misunderstood.

"Look here!" said Merle bluntly one day. "*Why*, I ask, *why* should people be expected to make such a fuss over you? I don't wonder you're neglected! I'd neglect you myself! And serve you jolly well right too!"

Whereupon Sybil dissolved into tears, and confided to her nearest friend that so long as Merle Ramsay was monitress she was afraid she would never be happy at 'The Moorings.' Poor Sybil had her good points. She was generous in her own way, and rather affectionate, but nature had not endowed her with tact, and she would go blundering on, never seeing that she was making mistakes. Her very chums soon tired of her and discreetly left her to some one else.

"I sometimes think she's a little bit dotty!" opined Nesta.

"Nonsense! She's as sane as you or I. It's all swank! I've no particular patience with her!" said Merle.

One particularly aggravating feature of Sybil was the way she traded upon rather delicate health. There was really nothing much the matter with her, but she sometimes had slight attacks of faintness, which, the girls declared, always came on when she thought she could be a subject of interest. She liked to extract sympathy from Miss Mitchell, or to arouse Miss Pollard's anxiety. Moreover, it was often a very good excuse for slacking off in her preparation or her practising.

One afternoon Merle, coming back to school, met Miss Mitchell by the gate.

"I was just looking for you!" said the teacher. "I've arranged an extra hockey practice at three, instead of English language. Will you tell the others?"

This was excellent news. The Fifth hated the English Language class, which consisted mostly of learning strings of horrible derivations, and to have it cut out for once in favour of hockey was quite an event. Merle walked up the drive smirking with satisfaction. By the porch she found Sybil, with an English language book in one hand, half-heartedly helping Miss Fanny, who was nailing up creepers. She looked very sorry for herself.

"I wish you'd hold the ladder, Merle!" she sighed, eager to thrust her duties on to a substitute. "I don't feel quite well this afternoon. I get such a faintness. Aren't these derivations too awful for anything?" she added *sotto voce*. "I don't believe I know one of them."

"Buck up!" whispered Merle with scant sympathy.

"It's all very well to say 'buck up'! You don't know what it is to feel faint. You're as strong as a horse. I'm really not fit to stand about!"

Angela Brazil

"Shall I ask Miss Fanny to let you go in and lie down?"

"I wish you would! I don't like to ask her myself; it seems making such a fuss."

Merle proffered the request, with which Miss Fanny, rather astonished, complied.

"Certainly, Sybil, if you really are ill! Shall I give you a dose of sal volatile?"

"No, thanks! I shall be all right if I can just rest on my bed," answered the plaintive voice.

"I daresay you'll soon feel better. It's a pity you'll miss the hockey practice," said Merle.

"What hockey practice?"

"Miss Mitchell has just told me to tell everybody. We're to play instead of having English language this afternoon."

Sybil's face was a study. But Miss Fanny's eyes were fixed upon her with such a questioning look that she was obliged to preserve her air of faintness and continue to pose as an invalid. There was nothing for it but to go and lie down. As she turned, however, she managed to whisper to Merle:

"You're the meanest thing on the face of this earth! Why couldn't you tell me sooner about the hockey?"

"Your own fault entirely!" chuckled Merle. "You nailed me straight away to do your job for you. Hope you'll enjoy yourself! Yes, Miss Fanny! I'm coming to hold the ladder! I was only opening the door for Sybil, she still-feels rather faint!"

It was about a week after this episode that Miss Mitchell, who was keen on nature study, took the Fifth form for a botanical ramble. They started punctually at two o'clock, so as to be back as soon as possible after four, on account of Beata Castleton and Fay Macleod, who must not keep Vicary's car waiting. They went off ready for business, all taking notebooks and pencils, some carrying tin cases, and some armed with boards with which to press their specimens on the spot. Their exodus was rather characteristic, for Aubrey was chatting sixteen to the dozen, Iva was trying to scoot ahead so as to walk alone with Kitty Trefyre, Muriel was squabbling with Merle as to which should appropriate Miss Mitchell, and Sybil was, as usual, seeking for sympathy.

"I couldn't find my boots! I had to put on my shoes instead, and the heels are worn down and they're not comfortable, and I shall very likely twist my ankle!" she complained. "What would you have done? Ought I to have gone to Miss Pollard and asked her about my boots?"

"And kept everybody waiting? You are the limit!" exclaimed Merle impatiently. "No, I'm not going to hold your case for you while you tie your hair ribbon. You always want to dump your things on to other people."

"You might carry the camera, at any rate!" wailed Sybil.

"Why should I? You insisted on bringing it, though I told you it would be a nuisance."

"It's for your benefit! I'm going to take a group of the whole party."

"Right-o! But don't expect to get the credit and make us carry the camera! You like to do your good deeds so cheaply!"

"Really, Merle!"

"I'm only telling you a few home truths. No, Mavis! I shan't let you load yourself with Sybil's property! You've got quite enough of your own to lug along!"

There was keen competition among the girls as to who could find most specimens. They rooted about in hedgerows, climbed banks, and made excursions into fields. Durracombe was not quite so good a neighbourhood for flowers as Chagmouth; still, they found a fair variety, and were able to chronicle early blooms of such specimens as the greater stitchwort, the ground ivy, and the golden saxifrage. It was a fresh March day, with a wind blowing scudding white clouds across a pale blue sky. Rooks were beginning to build, green foliage showed on the elder trees, and the elms were flowering.

"We shall all be pixie-led if we gather the white stitchwort!" said Mavis. "They're the pixies' flowers, so Mrs. Penruddock told me! It's a very old Devonshire superstition."

"Is that so? I never heard it before," said Miss Mitchell. "I know ever so many of the flowers are supposed to belong to the fairies in various parts of the country. Foxgloves are really 'the good folks' gloves,' and they're called fairies' petticoats in Cheshire, and fairies' hats in Ireland. Wild flax is always fairy flax, and harebells are fairy bells."

"Our old nurse used to call funguses pixie stools," said Edith Carey, "and the hollow ones were pixies' baths. She wouldn't let us pick elder, I can't remember why."

"That's a very old superstition. The 'elder mother' is supposed to live inside the tree, and to be very angry indeed if any harm is done to it. In the good old days, people used to ask her permission before they dared to cut down an elder. They knelt on bended knees and prayed:

"Lady Elder! Lady Elder!
Give me some of thy wood.

"There's a story about a man who hadn't the politeness to perform this little ceremony. He made a cradle for his baby out of the elder tree. But the sprite was offended, and she used to come and pull the baby out of the cradle by its legs, and pinch it and make it cry, so that it was quite impossible to leave the poor little thing in the elder cradle, and they had to weave one of basket-work for it instead."

"Tell us some more fairy lore about the plants!" begged the girls.

"Well, the St. John's wort is called 'the fairies' horse.' If you pick it after sunset a fairy horse will rise from the ground and carry you about all night, leaving you in the morning wherever you may chance to be at sunrise. You know if you keep fern-seed in your pockets you'll have the chance of seeing the pixies. The moonwort is supposed to be a very supernatural plant, and to have the power of opening locks if you place a leaf of it in the keyhole. No, I've never tried to burgle with it! I've never found any moonwort. It's an exceedingly rare plant now, and it's not been my luck to come across any. If you're troubled with warts, you ought to go at sunrise to an ash tree, stick a pin into the bark, and say:

> "Ashen tree! Ashen tree!
> I pray thee buy these warts of me!

"Then the ash tree would cure you, that's to say, if you'd repeated the charm properly!"

"I suppose it was always wise to leave a loophole in case the cure didn't come off!" laughed Mavis.

They had been walking by a footpath across the meadows, and found themselves in the little village of Bamberton, a small place with picturesque cottages close to a river. Miss Mitchell, who was an enthusiast upon architecture, marched her party off to view the church, much to the disgust of several of them.

"Don't want to see mouldy old churches! I'd rather be out of doors!" grumbled Merle.

"And there are actually sweet violets growing in a field on the

Angela Brazil

opposite side of the river," said Edith, who knew the neighbourhood.

"Oh, are there? Do let's get some."

"It'll be too late by the time we've been all round the monuments and read the inscriptions and the rest of it!"

"How long will Miss Mitchell stay in the church?"

"A good twenty minutes, I daresay. You can't get her away when she starts talking about architecture. Dad took her round our church one day, and I thought she'd never go. Tea was getting cold, but she went on asking questions about windows and pillars and things!"

"Then why shouldn't we slip out and run and get the violets while she's inside the church with the others?"

It was a naughty thing for a monitress to propose, but even Sybil, who happened to overhear, did not wax moral for the occasion.

"I'll come with you!" she said eagerly. "I'm not at all fond of going round churches, and looking at monuments. It always makes me wonder if I'm going to die young! When Miss Mitchell took us to Templeton Church and read us the epitaphs, I cried afterwards! There was one about a girl exactly my age. 'Sweet flower, nipped off in early bloom,' it said, or something of the sort."

"Don't be so sentimental!" snapped Merle.

"But come with us if you like. Yes, you too, Beata! But for goodness' sake don't tell any one else or they'll all want to come, and if the whole lot try to scoot, it will put a stopper on the thing. We'll wait till the others are inside and then just slide off. Mum's the word, though!"

It was quite easy to loiter among the tombstones pretending to read the inscriptions, but the moment Miss Mitchell and her audience had safely passed through the porch and opened the big nail-studded door, the four confederates turned and fled.

Edith knew a short cut, and took them between rows of graves, regardless of Sybil's protesting shudders, to a tiny stile that led down an alley to the riverside. Here there was a tumbledown wharf, and an old ferryboat which worked on a chain. Years ago a ferryman had had charge of it, but there was so little traffic that it was no longer worth his while, so the boat had been left for passengers to use as they liked. It was lying now at the edge of the wharf. The girls, following Edith, stepped in, and began to wind the boat across the river by pulling the chain. It was rather an amusing means of progression, and they enjoyed their 'Dover-Calais crossing,' as they called it. Arrived at the opposite bank, Edith scrambled out.

"Tie the boat up, somebody!" she called, and set off running over the meadow to the hedge where the violets grew.

Somebody is an exceedingly vague term, and generally means nobody. Merle and Beata went scampering after Edith, and Sybil, who was last, flung the boat chain hastily round a post and followed her friends. The violets were lovely, sweet-scented and blue and modest and everything that orthodox violets ought to be.

The girls gathered delicious, fragrant little bunches, and felt that they were scoring tremendously over those unfortunates who were receiving information about architecture inside the church.

"We mustn't stay too long!" sighed Edith. "It's a pity, but I'm afraid we really ought to go now. They'll be looking for us if we don't."

So they walked back across the meadow to the bank. Here a most unpleasant surprise greeted them. The boat, into which they had meant to step and ferry themselves back, had drifted into the middle of the river.

"Good gracious! Didn't you tie it up?" exclaimed Edith, aghast.

"Of course I did, but-well, I suppose I didn't tie it tight enough. I never thought it would float away," confessed Sybil.

The boat, though still working on the chain which spanned the river, was quite inaccessible from either side. The girls were in an extremely awkward position. Nobody knew where they had gone, and unless it occurred to some of their party to come and seek them by the wharf, or unless some chance passer-by happened to notice their plight, they might wait for a long time without rescue.

"What are we to do?" fumed Beata. "If we're not back at four the 'sardine-tin' will be waiting for me, and Mr. Vicary will be so cross! The last time we were late he went and complained to Father and said he'd have to charge us extra for wasting his time. There was an awful row, and Violet scolded Romola and me, although it was really Tattie's fault."

"Can we get to Durracombe on this side of the river?" suggested Sybil.

Edith shook her head.

"We could; but there isn't a bridge till you get to Parlingford, and that's five miles round. I think we'd better stay here."

"I could slay that wretched boat for playing us such a trick!" said Merle.

Meantime Miss Mitchell and the rest of the girls had finished their survey of the various monuments, and, catching sight of the church clock, realised how late it was, and that they must start back at once. Of course the four truants were missed, and a hasty search was made for them, in the chancel, and behind the organ, and outside among the tombstones.

"They're not anywhere here!" reported the scouts.

"Then they must have walked on," said Miss Mitchell. "Beata knew she had to be back by four o'clock. I expect we shall catch them up on the road. Come along!"

So the party set off at full speed, all unwitting that four disconsolate maidens were marooned on the farther side of the river, waiting for some faerie boat to ferry them across. For a long time no knight-errant arrived for their relief, but at last, as chance would have it, an urchin came down on to the wharf, with a string and a bent pin, intent on fishing. He was at least a link with the outer world, and they yelled hopefully to him across the water. He stopped and stared, then took to his heels and ran, but whether in terror or to fetch help they were uncertain. After what seemed a weary while, however, he returned, escorted by his father, who evidently understood the situation, for he shouted something which the girls could not catch, then went away.

"Has he left us to our fate?" asked Merle indignantly.

"Gone to get somebody else, perhaps!" ventured Edith more hopefully.

She proved correct, for after another eternity of time an old man hobbled on to the wharf, unlocked a boat-house, and slowly took out a punt, by means of which he reached the ferry-boat, climbed in, and worked it across the river to the farther bank.

"Why didn't 'ee fasten up the chain?" he asked; but as he was almost stone-deaf he did not understand either their excuses or professions of gratitude, and simply motioned to them to enter.

Arriving back on the wharf the girls, after subscribing a shilling amongst them to reward their rescuer, hurried up to the churchyard, where, of course, there was no sign of their party, then started as fast as they could to walk along the high road. They had gone perhaps half a mile when they heard a warning hoot behind them, and, looking round, what should Merle see but the little Deemster car with Dr. Tremayne at the driving-wheel. She shouted wildly and stopped him.

"Oh, Uncle David! Are you going back to Durracombe? Could you possibly take Beata at any rate! Her car will be waiting for her at school. We'd be everlastingly grateful!"

"I'll try and cram you all in if you like," smiled Dr. Tremayne. "Open the dickey, Merle!"

It was a decided squash. Edith and Sybil sat in front, and Merle and Beata managed to get together into the little dickey seat behind, where they each held one another in and clutched the hood for support.

"I have to pay a visit, but I'll run you back first," said Uncle David, setting off at a pace that made Merle and Beata cling for their lives as they whisked round corners. They arrived at 'The Moorings' exactly as the town-hall clock was chiming the quarter after four. Mr. Vicary, his face a study of patience, was standing by the side of the 'sardine-tin,' which was already packed for transit, and whose occupants set up a joyful screech of welcome.

"Of course, if Dr. Tremayne motored you back with Merle it's all right, though you ought to have asked me first," said Miss Mitchell, to whom Sybil gave a much edited explanation, omitting the ferry-boat incident altogether, and suppressing the violets.

So the four culprits, who had expected trouble, got off a great deal better than they deserved.

CHAPTER XII

FIFTH FORM JUSTICE

Easter was coming - Easter with its birds and flowers and hope of summer. Already there were hints of plans for the holidays, though these had not yet absolutely crystallised into shape. The mere mention of one of them had been enough to send Merle dancing round the house, but, as she had overheard by accident, and was strictly pledged not to reveal the secret to Clive, for the present she restrained her ecstasies and kept her lips sealed.

Meantime there was plenty to be done at school. The term-end examinations were due, and Miss Mitchell, who had been rather disappointed with Christmas results, was urging everybody to make heroic efforts. Mavis and Merle had missed much on account of the mumps, and when they attempted some revision they were absolutely appalled at the amount that had to be made up. They did their most creditable best, and toiled over text-books till heads ached. On the evening before the first examination they were sitting in Dr. Ramsay's study giving a farewell grind to several rather rusty subjects, when Clive walked in.

"Hello, kid! You're not allowed in here! We're working!" warned Merle.

Her young cousin grinned.

"I know! And you've got to stop it. I've been sent to tell you to shut those books up at once!"

"Did Mother say so?"

"She did. She says you've done enough, and you'll only muddle yourselves if you go on any longer."

"We shan't pass!" sighed Mavis.

"Yes, you will! Listen to the Oracle and he'll give you a tip or two. A little bird told him, look up Keltic words in the English language, and the life and works of William Cowper, and the products of Java and Borneo!"

Merle giggled.

"How clever you are all of a sudden! What do you know about our exam subjects?"

Clive winked solemnly, first with one eye and then with another.

"Perhaps I'm in communication with the occult!" he remarked. "Don't people go to clairvoyants and crystal-gazers and astrologers when they want to get tips about the future? I'm your wizard to-night."

"All right. Tell us our fortunes."

Clive reached over for the pack of Patience cards that Merle had left on the table, and shuffled them elaborately.

"The wizard is now ready to wizz. I may mention that my fee is only a guinea. You mustn't laugh or it might break the spell. Will you please to choose a card, look at it, and put it back in the pack."

"O Fate! wangle me a decent fortune!" chuckled Merle,

selecting at random. It was the six of spades, and her cousin shook his head gravely.

"That's a bad omen, but wait a bit! Stick it back in the pack and we'll see where it comes. Oh, this is better now-a dark woman is going to bring you trouble, but a fair man will come to the rescue and help you out. You're going amongst a number of people, but the general result will be fortunate. I see a number of diamonds, which means that prizes are in store for you."

"We don't have prizes at Easter! Is that all?"

"All that the cards tell me, but I'll do a little crystal-gazing if you like!" and Clive seized a glass paperweight, and, staring intently at it, pretended to throw himself into a state of abstraction.

"I see an examination-room!" he declared. "I see rows of desks, and girls writing at them. There are lists of questions. I am peeping over their shoulders, and they are puzzling about the products of Java and Borneo, and the life and works of William Cowper, and the Keltic words in the English language. You and Mavis are scribbling ahead for all you're worth."

"A very pretty picture, I'm sure! Can't you tell us some more?"

"Alas! The crystal has grown milky."

"And it's your bedtime!" said Mavis. "I expect you were on your way upstairs when you came in here. Confess!"

"There's no hurry. I'll stay and tell yours too if you like."

"No, thanks. This will do for both of us. Is Mother in the drawing-room? Come along, Merle, we won't work any more to-night."

"Oh, I must just look up what was it? - the products of Java and Borneo, and William Cowper, and Keltic words. There's luck in them! Just for five minutes! Get off to bed, you kid, and leave me to work."

Rather reluctantly Mavis fell in with her sister's humour and reopened her text-books.

"Clive's only fooling!" she remonstrated.

"I know; and so am I! Here we are - Keltic words in use in the English language. You can squint over my shoulder if you like."

The five minutes lengthened out till Mrs. Ramsay came herself and put a finish to the preparation.

"It's silly to overdo it. You'll only have headaches to-morrow and be able to remember nothing. Come along to the drawing-room and sing to Father."

"Yes, Mummie darling, I'm just strapping up my books. There, I'll leave them here on the hall-table. I promise you I won't take them upstairs. Hello! Here's my jersey! I was hunting for it everywhere after tea and couldn't find it. It feels wet! How funny! Has anybody been out in it?"

"Give it to Alice and ask her to put it by the kitchen fire to dry. Father wants to hear that Devon folksong you're learning. It will do you good to have a little music after such hard brain-work."

Merle marched into school next morning joking about her fortune. She told the girls what the oracle had said, and how she had ground up those particular bits of information.

"I'm sporting enough to give you the tip!" she laughed.

"Clive was only making fun and ragging us!" qualified Mavis.

"He's a silly boy."

There was no time for any more last looks, however. The bell was ringing for call-over, and all books must be put away. In the Fifth form room a clean sheet of blotting-paper was laid upon every desk, and the inkwells had been newly filled. Miss Mitchell dealt round typewritten sheets of questions, and the agony began. The English Language and Literature paper was not nearly so bad as Mavis and Merle had expected, and curiously enough there were questions both on William Cowper and on Keltic words. It was such a coincidence that Merle could not help looking at Mavis and smiling. They were both well prepared, and wrote away at full speed, almost enjoying themselves, and worked steadily till Miss Mitchell said, "Pens down." After eleven o'clock came the examination on the text-book geography, which had this term - owing to Miss Pollard's influence - supplemented the lantern lectures on that subject. When she saw the first question, "Describe the products of Java and Borneo," Merle gave such an audible chuckle that many eyes were cast in her direction, and Miss Mitchell glared a warning. Again Mavis and Merle found themselves well prepared, and scribbled continuously till the bell rang.

"How did you get on?" said Merle to Muriel, as they walked downstairs from their classroom. "I say! Wasn't it funny about my fortune? Why, we had the exact questions! I never heard of anything so queer in my life!"

"Very queer!" answered Muriel, with restraint in her voice. She was looking at Iva, who shrugged her shoulders significantly.

"Some people have all the luck!" remarked Sybil.

"Well, it was lucky, for it was pure guessing of Clive's."

"How did he know what exams you were going to have?"

"Oh, he's heard us talking about them, of course."

"I wish I had a cousin who could guess the questions beforehand."

"We'd all get Honours on those lines."

When Mavis and Merle returned to school after lunch, they each found a little note laid upon their desks marked 'Urgent.'

> You are requested to attend a most important meeting to be held in the boarders' sitting-room at the hostel immediately after four.

There was no signature, but the writing was Iva's. The Ramsays were much mystified. As day-girls they had nothing to do with the hostel, and could only go there by special invitation. When afternoon school was over they asked some of the boarders the meaning of the missive. Nobody would explain.

"You'll find out when you get there," was Nesta's cryptic reply.

Puzzled, and considerably distressed at a certain offensive attitude exhibited by Sybil and others, Mavis and Merle walked across the garden to the hostel. Iva had cleared all the younger girls out of the boarders' sitting-room, and was waiting in company with Nesta, Muriel, Aubrey, Edith, and Kitty. As soon as the Ramsays and Sybil came in, she closed the door.

"I've called a general meeting of the Fifth," she said, "because there's something we all feel we ought to go into. Would you like to elect some one into the chair?"

"I beg to propose yourself," piped Aubrey.

"And I beg to second," said Nesta.

Iva settled herself and looked somewhat embarrassed, as if not knowing quite how to begin. She fidgeted for a moment with her pencil, and cleared her throat.

"We're all here," she said at last, "except Fay and Beata, who couldn't stay. What we've met for is to ask Mavis and Merle to explain how it was they got to know some of the examination questions beforehand. It seems to us queer, to say the least of it!"

The Ramsays, overwhelmed with amazement at such a palpable insinuation, turned wrathfully red.

"Why, we've told you! Clive guessed!" gasped Merle.

"Bunkum!"

"How could he?"

"Very convenient guessing, I'm sure!"

"It's no use telling us such utter fibs!"

"They're not fibs! How dare you say so!" flamed Merle.

"It's the absolute truth!" endorsed Mavis.

"Do you stick to that?"

"Of course we do."

"Then I shall have to call on Sybil to tell us something she saw yesterday."

Sybil, who was red, nervous, and even more uncomfortable than Iva, rose from her seat to make her accusation.

"I was in the garden yesterday after school, and I saw Merle come back, hurry among the bushes, and climb in at the study window. I waited, and presently she came out again and scooted off as if she didn't want to meet anybody."

"O - o - oh! You *didn't* see me! I wasn't there! Was I, Mavis?"

"Most certainly not. You were at home all the time. I can prove that!"

"I think the thing proves itself!" said Iva. "First of all, you're seen by a witness entering the study, where, no doubt, the exam papers were spread out on the table, and then you come to school primed with the questions. There isn't a shadow of doubt."

"Wait a minute!" said Mavis, rising with a very white face. "To begin with, you've got to prove that it was Merle. One witness isn't enough."

"Catie and Peggie saw her down the drive. They told me so."

"What time was it?"

"About five o'clock."

"She was practising at home then. I can bring witnesses to prove that. Besides, if she had really seen the questions, do you think she'd have been silly enough to tell them to you before the exam?"

The girls looked puzzled at that, but Nesta murmured that Merle was silly enough for anything.

"As she's one of the monitresses, we thought we ought to give her a chance to clear herself before we told Miss Mitchell," said Iva.

"She *can* clear herself and she will. It's not fair to condemn her like this. You must give her time to bring her own witnesses. I ask you all, is it like Merle to do such a thing?"

"Well, no, it certainly isn't like either of you. That's what's surprised us so much."

"You feel you can't be sure of anybody," added Aubrey.

The boarders' tea-gong, sounding at that moment, brought the meeting to an unsatisfactory conclusion. The Ramsays hurried home, bubbling over with indignation, to pour their woes into Mother's sympathetic ear, and were highly put out to find the drawing-room full of callers, and to be expected to hand tea-cups and make pleasant conversation instead of retailing their grievances. They beat a retreat as soon as they possibly could, and, for fear of being asked to play or sing for the benefit of visitors, deemed it wise to escape into the garden.

"We'll sit in the summer-house, only I must have my jersey," declared Merle, catching up the garment in question from its peg in the hall, and pulling it on. "I want some place where I can explode. This is just the beastliest thing that's ever happened to me in all my life."

"I can't understand it!" puzzled Mavis, with her forehead in wrinkles.

Merle was stumping along the path with her hands in the pockets of her jersey.

"Why should they accuse *me*, of all people in the world, of climbing in through the study window? Sybil must have been dreaming. She's an idiot of a girl. She'd imagine anything from a ghost to a burglar. What are we going to do about it? I wish to goodness they *would* tell Miss Mitchell! I'd rather she knew. I've a jolly good mind to go and tell her myself. Then I should have first innings and she'd hear our side of it. Hello! There's Clive."

It was that lively young gentleman who came walking along the garden wall and took a flying leap on to the path, just avoiding one of Tom's best flower-beds.

"There's a whole tribe of ladies in the drawing-room!" he volunteered. "I carried my tea into the summer-house! You won't catch me 'doing the polite' if I can help it. Rather not! Have you bunked too? I don't blame you. You're looking down in the mouth, both of you! Exams gone wrong this afternoon? Shall I tell your fortunes again?"

"Your precious fortune has got us into a great deal of trouble," answered Merle. "How did you manage to guess those questions? They were actually in our papers!"

Clive pulled his face into a variety of grimaces.

"Ah! Wouldn't you just like to know!" he retorted. "Perhaps I keep a familiar spirit, or perhaps I read things in the stars. I prophesy you'll fail in all the rest of your exams! There!"

"You young wretch!" cried Merle, chasing him down the path as he fled. She took her hands from her pockets to catch hold of him, and as she did so out flew a penknife on to the grass. Clive pounced upon it immediately and picked it up.

"I've been looking for this everywhere!" he declared.

"How did it get inside my pocket?" asked Merle.

"*I* never put it there!"

"Clive!" exclaimed Mavis, with a sudden flash of intuition. "Did you wear Merle's jersey yesterday? I remember she found it wet. I verily believe you dressed up in her clothes and went to school."

For answer Clive burst into fits of laughter.

"Oh, it was topping!" he hinnied. "I stuck on her skirt and jersey and tam o' shanter and took in everybody. I walked down the street, and up the drive to the school door, and prowled round the garden. There was a window open, so in I went and found exam questions all over the table. I thought I'd rag you about them!"

"You atrocious imp! Look here! You don't know what a scrape you've got us into. You'll just have to own up and get us out of it again, that's all!"

Irresponsible Clive was full of thoughtless mischief, and it was a long time before the girls could get him to see the serious side of his escapade, and realise what an exceedingly grave charge had been brought against their honour. In the end, by dint of scolding, entreaty, coercion, and even bribery, they succeeded in persuading him to come along with them to 'The Moorings,' where they asked for Miss Mitchell, and told her the whole story.

"I'm extremely glad to know," she said, looking hard at Clive. "The fact is I was deceived myself. He's very like you, Merle! I happened to see him climbing out of the window, and I certainly thought I recognised you. I've felt upset all day about it. I couldn't understand your doing such a thing."

"Will you explain to the boarders, please! I hate them to think me a sneak."

"I'll make that all right."

"And about those exam questions - Mavis and I wouldn't have dreamt of looking them up beforehand, and I don't suppose we should have known them. Wouldn't it be fairer just to cross them off in our papers and not count them? We'd much rather you did."

"Yes, it's the only thing to be done."

Clive, much subdued, blurted out a kind of apology before he left, which Miss Mitchell accepted with dignity. Perhaps she did not think it good for him to forgive him too easily. His evil prophecies about the exams were fortunately not fulfilled, for his cousins, though they did not score brilliant successes, just managed to scrape through without any failures.

　　　　Angela Brazil

The Fifth form, when they heard the true facts of the story, repented their hasty court of justice and made handsome amends.

"It doesn't matter!" said Merle. "You were quite right if you thought we'd been cheating. I should pull anybody else up myself, fast enough. It must have been the acting we did at Christmas that put the idea into Clive's idiotic young head. He was dressed up as a girl then, and rather fancied himself. He really is the limit."

"We shall always be a little uncertain now which is you and which is your cousin!" laughed Iva.

"Oh, he won't do it again! We've put him on his honour, and I don't think he'd break his word."

CHAPTER XIII

THE KITTIWAKE

The great Easter secret, which Merle had surprised and preserved with so much difficulty, was out at last. Clive's father and mother were coming to Devonshire for a holiday; they had taken rooms at a farm in Chagmouth, and they had not only arranged for their own son to join them, but they had also asked Mavis and Merle to be their visitors. The girls thought that no invitation could have been more delightfully acceptable. They adored Chagmouth, and the Saturdays they managed to spend there were always red-letter days, so the prospect of three whole weeks in this El Dorado sent their spirits up to fizzing-over point.

"Bevis will be at Grimbal's Farm!"

"And Tudor will be at home!"

"The Castletons are expecting Morland and Claudia!"

"And, of course, Fay will be there, and Tattie, and the Colvilles!"

"Goody! What a lovely tribe of us to go out picnics!"

"We'll have the time of our lives!"

Burswood Farm, where Mr. and Mrs. Percy Tremayne had

Angela Brazil

taken rooms, was on the hillside above Chagmouth. It was a delightful spot, with that airy feeling about it that comes from looking down upon your neighbours' chimneys.

"I wouldn't live in Chagmouth, not if you paid me hundreds a year!" declared Mrs. Treasure, their landlady. "Once I'm up here, here I stay! I've not been in the town for over six months. I go on Sundays to the little chapel close by, and if I want shops we get out the gig and drive into Kilvan or Durracombe. It isn't worth the climb back from Chagmouth. I carried William up when he was a baby, and it nearly killed me. I set him down in his cradle and I said: 'There, my boy! I don't go down to Chagmouth again till you can walk back yourself!' And I didn't! He was three years old before I went - even to the post office. How do I manage about stamps? Why, the postman brings them for me and takes my letters. The grocers' carts come round from Kilvan, and the butcher calls once a week, and what can you want more? I say when I've got a nice place like this to live in I'll stay here, and not worry myself with climbing up and down hill."

Though Mavis and Merle might not hold with Mrs. Treasure's depreciation of Chagmouth, they thoroughly agreed with her eulogy of Burswood. There was a view of the sea from the farm, and it had an old-fashioned garden with beehives and hedges of fuchsia and blue veronica, and at the back there was a small fir wood, with clumps of primroses and opening bluebells. The girls christened it 'Elfland.'

"You can almost see the fairies here," said Mavis. "Why is it that some places feel so much more romantic than others?"

"Because you're in the right mood, I suppose. This is almost as nice as Blackthorn Bower."

"Not quite. Nothing can ever come up to that! When Bevis gets The Warren he's going to build up the Bower again."

"Why doesn't he do it now? The Glyn Williams would let him

if he wanted. It's his property."

"He wouldn't care to ask them; especially after what happened there between him and Tudor."

"They've forgotten that, surely!"

"Well, I sympathise with Bevis. He doesn't care to interfere with anything until The Warren is really his own. I think he feels they'd laugh at the Bower, and so they would!"

"It's not in their line, of course."

However much we may love old and familiar scenes, there is always a novelty in something new, and the bird's-eye aspect of Chagmouth was attractive, especially to those whose young limbs did not mind the climb. Mr. and Mrs. Percy Tremayne were most enthusiastic about their quarters. They were charming people, and ready to fall in with the young folk's plans and give them a thoroughly happy holiday. They had brought a motor-bicycle and side-car, and took some excursions round the neighbourhood, going over often to Durracombe to see Dr. and Mrs. Tremayne, glad to have the opportunity of a private chat with them while their lively son was safely picnicking with Mavis and Merle. Picnics were the established order of the day. The girls declared that Society at Chagmouth this Easter began with a big S. The Castletons were a host in themselves. They were all at home, and all equally fascinating. Musical Mavis attached herself to Claudia with a great admiration, and Merle found a devoted knight in ten-year-old Madox, who clung to her with the persistency of a chestnut burr, chiefly because she had the charity to answer his perpetual questions. "The interrogation mark," as he was called by his own family, was a typical Castleton, and most cherubic of countenance, though his curls had been sheared in deference to school, spoiling him, so his father declared, for artistic purposes. He was a mixture of mischief and romance, and Merle, who accepted his temporary allegiance, never quite knew whether his embraces were marks of genuine affection or were designed for the chance of dropping pebbles down her back.

Some delightful friends of the Castletons were also spending a holiday in rooms at Chagmouth - Miss Lindsay, an artist, and Lorraine Forrester, a chum of Claudia's, both of whom were sketching the quaint streets and the quay and the harbour with the wildest enthusiasm. Morland had also taken a sudden fancy for painting, and insisted upon going out with them daily, producing some quite pretty little impressionistic pictures, with a touch of his father's style about them. In Morland the family talent ran high but never rose to genius. His touch on the piano was perfect. He scribbled poems in private. His achievements, however, in either music, art, or poetry were insufficient to justify taking one of them for a vocation.

"I'd rather make him a chimney-sweep!" declared Mr. Castleton eloquently. "The public nowadays don't appreciate pictures! They'll look at them in galleries, especially when the admission is free, but you can't get them to buy. They hang their drawing-rooms with cheap prints instead of water-colours, and go to the photographers instead of the portrait-painter. If you can design something to advertise mustard or cocoa you may make a little money, but not by pure art! It's as dead as the ancient Greeks. This is a commercial age. Music's as bad. Your pianists are glad to take posts to play at the cinemas! I wish Claudia success; but her training is the business of the college, not mine, and *they'll* have to bring her out. I've nothing to do with it. No; Morland must realise he's living in the twentieth century, and has to earn his bread and butter. Art doesn't pay, and that's the fact! Have it as a hobby if you wish, but don't depend upon it!"

So Morland, who, like many young fellows of artistic calibre, had a general affection for the muses but no very marked vocation for anything, had been pitchforked into engineering, and was making quite tolerable progress, and would possibly support himself later on, but always with the feeling that life was commonplace and unromantic, and that a splendid vision had been somewhere just round the corner, only unfortunately missed. He allowed his artistic temperament to run loose during the holidays. He would go up to Bella Vista and play for hours on the Macleods' new grand piano, improvising beautiful airs, and sending Fay into raptures.

"Why don't you write them down right away?" she demanded.

"What's the use? No one would publish them if I did. The publishers are fed up with young composers wanting a hearing. I've made up my mind to be just an amateur - nothing more."

"I'm not sure," ventured Mrs. Macleod, "whether you won't have the best of it. After all, 'amateur' means 'lover,' and the art and the music that you pursue for pure pleasure will be more to you than what you might have had to produce for the sake of bread and butter. Why must our standard in these things always be the commercial one, 'does it pay?' The fact of making it pay often degrades it. My theory is that a man can have his business, and love his hobby just as he loves his wife, without turning it into L s. d. Look at my husband! In his own office there isn't any one in America knows more about motor fittings, but once outside the office his heart and soul is in painting. I believe he's a happier man for doing both!"

"Do you really think so? It cheers me up! When I'm a full-blown engineer, perhaps I'll make enough to buy a grand piano at any rate. That's one way of looking at it. It's awfully kind of you to let me come here and thump away on yours."

"We enjoy having you, so use it whenever you like. It's always absolutely at your disposal."

Morland was not the only one of the party who was amusing his leisure hours. Bevis also had hobbies. He had taken up photography, had turned an attic at Grimbal's Farm into a dark room, and was trying many experiments. Moreover, his lawyers had at last yielded to his urgent entreaties and had

Angela Brazil

allowed him to buy a small sailing yacht. She was not a racing craft, or remarkably smart in any way, but she was his own, and the joy of possession was supreme. He rechristened her The Kittiwake, painting in her new name with much satisfaction, and he made trial trips in her along the coast as far as Port Sennen. He was extremely anxious to take Mavis and Merle and Clive with him, but that was strictly prohibited by Mrs. Tremayne, who would not allow either her son or her visitors to venture.

"It's too big a risk, and I know what Clive is! Young Talland can swim like a fish if he upsets his yacht, but *you* can't!"

"We can swim!" protested Merle.

"A little, close by the shore, I daresay, but that's nothing if you're plunged into deep water. I can't take the responsibility of letting you go. Never mind! We'll make up a party one day and take a motor-boat with a proper experienced boatman. Young Talland can join us then if he likes."

Mavis and Merle were disappointed almost to the point of tears. They had duly admired *The Kittiwake* in the harbour, and they simply longed to go on board. It seemed so particularly tempting when they had such a cordial invitation, and so aggravating to be obliged to decline.

"Cousin Nora's very nervous," urged Mavis in extenuation. "She'd be afraid of our being drowned if we went on a duck-pond."

Bevis passed over the slur on his seamanship.

"It's all right!" he answered quietly, but there was a certain set obstinate look about his mouth which the girls knew well, and which meant that he intended if possible to get his own way, though he said nothing more at the time.

It was perhaps as well for everybody's peace of mind that he should not take Clive boating, for the boy was venturesome and mischievous, and rather out of hand except when his father was by. He often made the girls' hair almost stand on end by his pranks at the verge of the cliffs, and was sometimes the cause of considerable bad language among the sailors when he interfered with their nets or tar-pots down on the quay. It was a relief to Mavis and Merle when Mr. Tremayne took him out in the side-car, and they knew that for some hours at least they need not be responsible for his behaviour. They were both fond of botany, and were enthusiastically making collections of wild flowers to press for their holiday task. Bevis was a good ally in this respect, and would often call in at Burswood Farm with some uncommon specimen which he thought they had not yet found for themselves. He had come on this errand one morning, and was helping Mavis to screw up her pressing boards, when Mrs. Tremayne happened to mention the scarcity of shells in the neighbourhood of Chagmouth.

"I've hardly found any!" she remarked. "And I'm so annoyed, because it happens to be my particular hobby. I'm collecting them. I suppose the coast is too rocky and they get broken. They're always very local things."

"There's just one place I know where you might find some," said Bevis. "It's a particular patch of sand near Gurgan Point. I saw some beauties there a while ago. I'll show you where it is with pleasure if you like."

"Oh, thanks! That would be delightful," beamed Mrs. Tremayne. "The girls and I could go to-day if you can take us. My husband and Clive are out with the motor-bike, so it's a splendid opportunity."

"Let me see! The tide should be just right this afternoon," agreed Bevis cheerfully. "Mavis and Merle know the way to Gurgan Point. If they'll take you there and down the path to the cove, I'll come round in the yacht and meet you. Shall we say at three o'clock?"

"That would be exactly nice time after lunch."

"Very well, I'll be there."

Bevis went back to Grimbal's Farm chuckling to himself, though he did not betray the cause of his amusement to anybody. He hunted out a hamper and packed it with cups and saucers, a methylated spirit-lamp, and other picnic requisites. On his way to the quay he stopped at the confectioner's and bought cakes and fancy biscuits. He placed these comestibles inside the hamper, and stowed it away in the locker of *The Kittiwake*. At two o'clock he was out of the harbour, and was off in the direction of Gurgan Point.

Mavis and Merle and Cousin Nora, bearing baskets in which to place shells, had a pleasant walk along the cliffs, and descended the path to the trysting-place. They found Bevis waiting for them in the cove. He had moored *The Kittiwake* to a buoy, and now led the way over the sands to a sort of little peninsula that jutted out into the sea. Here he had beached his dinghy.

"This is the shell-bank. You'll find heaps of them here!" he said.

Undoubtedly he had brought them to the right place. There were shells in abundance, and of many different kinds, delicate pink ones, tiny cowries, twisted wentletraps, scallops, screw-shells, and some like mother-of-pearl. Mrs. Tremayne was in raptures, and went down on her knees to gather them. There was such a tempting variety that it was difficult to stop, and in the excitement of the quest the time simply fled.

"I haven't brought my watch!" declared Mrs. Tremayne once.

"Oh, it's quite early yet!" Bevis assured her. "I've lighted the spirit-lamp, and I'm going to make you some tea."

He had carried the hamper on to the sands, and was busy

setting out his cups and saucers in a sheltered place behind some rocks, 'to be out of the wind,' as he carefully explained. When his kettle boiled he filled the tea-pot, and summoned his guests.

"You've chosen a snug spot!" said Mrs. Tremayne, walking along with her eyes on the sands still looking for shells.

And Merle, who was watching a white line of advancing waves, added:

"Lovely and snug, only I hope we shan't get -"

She meant to say 'surrounded,' but Bevis pulled such a fearful face at her behind Cousin Nora's back that she stopped short and let him finish the sentence.

"We shan't get shells while we're having tea, of course! You can look for some more afterwards if you haven't enough."

"Oh, surely, we have heaps and heaps! And simply exquisite ones! These tiny yellow babies are just perfect. I like them better than the big grandfathers," exulted Mavis.

Bevis made a polite but leisurely host. He insisted on boiling some more water, which was not really wanted, but which took a long time, and he spun out his own tea interminably.

"It's so jolly here under the rocks!" he declared. "I like the *dolce far niente* - makes one think of lotus-eaters and all the rest of it. Shall I help you sort your shells? You could wash them in the tea-cups. It's no use carrying home surplus sand. There's some water left in the kettle."

On one pretext or another he kept them dawdling under the rocks, till Mrs. Tremayne at last rose up and declared they really must be starting back for the cove.

"We shall be having the tide coming in if we don't mind," she said. "Why! Look!"

She might well exclaim, for while they had been sitting with their backs to the sea the water had all the while been lapping slowly in and had changed their peninsula into an island. They were entirely surrounded, and quite a wide channel lay between themselves and the shore. Mrs. Tremayne looked much alarmed, but Bevis took the matter with the utmost calm.

"It's all right! I've the dinghy here, and I can row you to the yacht. I'd land you in the cove if I could, but it really wouldn't be safe because of the rocks. I'll sail you all back to Chagmouth and run you into the harbour."

There was evidently nothing else to be done, and though Cousin Nora might not enjoy the prospect of yachting, she was obliged to accept Bevis's offer.

It was quite a pleasant little excursion from Gurgan Point to the harbour; the sea was luckily calm, but there was sufficient breeze to enable The Kittiwake to skim over the water like her sea-gull namesake. The girls, who by this time had grasped the depths of their friend's plot, enjoyed the situation immensely. They were actually having their coveted sail in the very company of the dear lady who had so expressly forbidden the jaunt, and all without the slightest friction or trouble. Bevis, indeed, was posing as rescuer and accepting grateful thanks.

"It's a lesson to us all to watch the tide and not sit talking with our backs to the sea!" said Cousin Nora virtuously.

"It is indeed!" answered Bevis, so gravely that Merle had to stuff her handkerchief into her mouth to stifle her chortles of mirth.

He brought them into the harbour, and helped them to land on the steps of the jetty.

"Wasn't I clever?" he whispered, as he handed Mavis her basket of shells. "When I really make up my mind to get a thing, I get it!"

Angela Brazil

CHAPTER XIV

THE HAUNTED TREE

There were so many jolly friends staying at Chagmouth at present that they made a most delightful circle. Generally they all managed to meet every day, and the usual trysting-place was The Haven, partly because it was in so central a situation for everybody, but chiefly because the kind-hearted, unconventional Castletons were ready at any and every time to welcome visitors, and would allow friends to 'drop in' in true Bohemian fashion, quite regardless of whatever happened to be taking place in the household. From the studio, indeed, they were excluded while Mr. Castleton was at his easel, but they were allowed to use it when he was not working, and it proved admirable for either games, theatricals, or dancing. With so many costumes in the cupboard it was easy to get up charades, and they had much fun over acting. Perhaps the most successful was a small performance of 'The Babes in the Wood,' given by the Castleton children, with Perugia and Gabriel, lovely in Elizabethan costume, as 'the babes' John and Jane; Madox and Constable as the two villains 'Daggersdrawn' and 'Triggertight,' who abandoned them in the wood; and Lilith as the beneficent fairy 'Dewdrop,' who found them and whisked them away to bonny Elfland. The little Castletons had natural dramatic instincts and were adepts at posing, so their play was really very pretty. Madox, in especial, absolutely excelled himself as a robber and came out tremendously. He bowed gallantly in response to the storm of applause, and blew an airy kiss to Merle, who nearly collapsed with mirth. She thought her ten-year-old admirer deserved something in return for so graceful an attention, so she sent him a box of chocolates with a few verses written on a sheet of paper and placed inside.

TO DAGGERSDRAWN

You're a very handsome fellow,
So gallant and so gay;
And I really blush to tell you,
But you've stole my heart away.

When you took the part of Daggersdrawn,
My bosom swelled with pride
To hear your voice of thunder
And see your manly stride.

You seized the nasty pistols up
Without a sign of fear,
And thrust and parried with your sword
Just like a Cavalier.

As you've escaped the lonesome wood -
For so the story ends -
I send these chocs, with best regards,
And beg we may be friends.

Merle had no doubt the chocolates would be appreciated, but she had not expected to receive back a poetical effusion from her small knight. He evidently, however, had some slight gift for minstrelsy, for one day there was a tremendous rap on the front-door knocker at Burswood Farm, then a sound of running footsteps, and inside the letter-box was a note addressed to 'Miss Merle Ramsay,' in a rather wobbly and unformed hand. At the top of the sheet of paper was painted a boat with brown sails on a blue sea, and underneath was written:

You ask me, dear, will I be thine?
How can you such a question ask

When, 'neath the robber's fearful mask,
I languish for thee, lady mine!

Thou art the lady that I love;
Thou art the lady that I chose.
Oh, fly with me from friends and foes!
Oh, for the wings of a dove!

O sail with me to a southern sea,
To where an isle is fair and warm,
And the sea around it bright and calm:
O Merle, will you come with me?

But for the nasty pistols, miss,
I have one ready to shoot me dead!
For already my heart is heavy as lead
Unless you favour my wish!

[Footnote: These verses were really composed by a little boy.]

 It's rather silly but it's the best I can rite. M C.

In the privacy of the parlour Merle had a good laugh with
Mavis over what they termed her first love-letter.

"'Oh, for the wings of a dove!'" quoted Merle. "It's so Biblical,
isn't it? He's a dear, all the same! I love him better even than
Constable. He's such a bright little chap. Don't tell Clive, or
he'd tease Madox to death about this. It must be an absolute
secret. I can just picture the child sitting writing it with his
sticky little fingers!"

"You mustn't let him know about 'Sweet William,' or there'll
be a free fight!" laughed Mavis.

William was Mrs. Treasure's little boy, and also an ardent
admirer of Merle, who gave him chocolates when she met him
in the garden or the stackyard. In spite of his mother's
injunctions to 'Behave and not trouble the visitors,' he would

hang about the passages to present Merle with handfuls of ferns and flowers grabbed at random from the hedgerows and of no botanical value whatever; or sometimes the parlour window would be cautiously opened from the outside, a pair of bright eyes would appear, and a small grubby hand would push in a bird's egg or some other country trophy as an offering. It was William who told Merle about the 'headless horseman,' a phantom rider who was reported to gallop down the road after dusk, and whom Chagmouth mothers found useful as a bogey to frighten their children with.

"He'll get you if you're out when it's dark!" said William, with round awed eyes.

"What would he do with you if he did?" asked Merle.

But such a pitch of horror was beyond the limit of William's imagination, and he could only reaffirm his original statement.

Of course the girls and Clive were very excited to learn that a real live ghost was supposed to haunt the neighbourhood. They discussed it at the dinner-table over the jam-tart and cream.

"We've certainly heard a sort of trotting sound when we've been in bed at night," said Mavis, anxious to establish evidence. "We didn't think of getting up to look out of the window, but I don't suppose we could have seen on to the road if we had."

"Yes; I remember people used to believe in the 'headless horseman,'" said Mr. Tremayne, who had known Chagmouth very well as a boy. "There was a demon dog, too, that ran down Tinkers' Lane, and an old lady who 'walked' by the well."

A delighted howl arose from the family at the mention of two more spooks.

"O - o - h! Tell us about the demon dog!" implored Clive.

"It had eyes as big as saucers, and they shone like fire. It used to scuttle along the lane, and no one ever waited to see where it went, though there used to be a hole in a bank where I was told it had once disappeared."

"Was it *really* ever seen?" asked Merle.

"I believe all these phantoms were clever devices of the smugglers in the old days, when it was very desirable to have the roads quiet at night in order to carry about contraband goods. It would be quite easy to fake a demon dog. You take a black retriever, fasten two cardboard circles smeared with phosphorus round his eyes, give him a kick, and send him running down a dark road, and every one who met him would have hysterics. As for the headless horseman, that's also a well-known smugglers' dodge - false shoulders can be made and fixed on a level with the top of your head, and covered with a cloak, so that the apparently headless man has eyes in the middle of his chest, and can see to ride uncommonly well. It was generally to somebody's interest to make up these ghosts and frighten people."

"You take all the romance out of it!" pouted Mavis.

In spite of Mr. Tremayne's most reasonable explanations they clung to the supernatural side of the stories. It was much more interesting to picture the demon dog as the property of his Satanic Majesty, than to believe it an ordinary black retriever with circles of phosphorus round its eyes.

"I vote we go and try and see it for ourselves!" suggested Clive, waxing bold one evening. The girls agreed, so just before bedtime they sallied forth in the direction of Tinkers' Lane, a lonely stretch of road that led from the hillside towards the sea. They were all three feeling half valiant and half scared, and each had brought some species of protection. Mavis carried a prayer-book and a little ivory cross, Merle grasped a poker, and

Clive was armed with the hatchet from the wood-pile. So long as they were on the uplands and could see the stars they marched along tolerably bravely, but presently Tinkers' Lane turned downhill, and, like most of its kind in Devon, ran between high fern-grown banks, on the tops of which grew trees whose boughs almost met overhead and made an archway. To plunge down here was like taking a dip into Dante's 'Inferno,' it looked so particularly dark and gloomy, and such a suitable place for anything ghostly.

"I wish we'd brought a lantern with us!" murmured Mavis.

"Then we shouldn't see any spooks!" declared Merle. "Come along! Let's go as far as the old gate at any rate. I dare you both to come! Who's afraid?"

Clive certainly was not going to show the white feather, and Mavis, though rather nervy, preferred to venture forward with the others than to remain by herself, so it ended in their all going on, arm-in-arm. They had worked themselves to such a pitch of excitement that the whole atmosphere seemed charged with the supernatural. There were mysterious groanings and rustlings in the hedge, and the long branches of the trees moaned as they swayed. It was so dark they were almost groping their way, and could barely see the banks on either side. Suddenly, through a rift in the trees came a faint gleam of starlight, and oh! horror of horrors! What was that black dog-like object running rapidly towards them up the lane? Mavis, whose over-sensitive nerves were strung up to the last point, yelled with terror, and clung screaming to Merle, who gave a shriek of agony herself as the phantom approached and leaped at them.

"Whatever's the matter?" cried a voice, and a figure came hurrying forward and flashed an electric torch upon the scene.

In the circle of light thus formed the girls saw nothing more alarming than Bevis and his spaniel Fan, who was jumping up affectionately at Merle and licking her hands. They drew long

Angela Brazil

breaths and then laughed.

"They thought you were Old Nick himself and his demon dog!" vouchsafed Clive, very brave now the alarm was over.

"What are you all doing down Tinkers' Lane so late as this?" asked Bevis.

"We came out to see spooks!"

"You won't find anything worse than Fan and myself! Better let us take you home."

"Oh, I wish you would," said Mavis, accepting the escort with alacrity. "I don't think I like this dark place. I'm rather scared still. I don't wonder people see bogeys here. If you'd been riding, Bevis, I should certainly have taken you for the headless horseman. He rides here, doesn't he?"

"I'll tackle him for you if we meet him, never fear!" laughed Bevis. "I'll tell him it isn't respectable to go about without a head, and he must put it on again at once! All the same, though" (more gravely), "I think, if I were you, I wouldn't come down this lane in the dark all by yourselves."

"We certainly shan't!"

"It's a good thing I didn't use the hatchet on poor Fan," said Clive, forbearing to mention that he had been huddling in the hedge, much too paralysed to take such violent measures.

"Bless her! She's an angel dog - not a demon!" murmured Merle, fondling the silky ears that pressed close to her dress. "But you gave your auntie rather a scare, darling! Another time you mustn't bounce upon her in the dark! You must be a good girlie, and remember!"

The adventurous trio were not at all sorry to be taken safely to their own gateway by Bevis, but all the same they felt a little disappointed that they had no real peep at phantom forms in the lane. The girls did not intend to tell their experience to William, but Clive let it out, so they had to give him the full account. He looked at them with awe-struck admiration.

"Suppose it had really been the ghost and it had got you!" he ventured.

William took the supernatural side of life seriously. It was no laughing matter to him. On the very next day he came to Merle with important news.

"There's something queer in the wood above the house. I was up there with Connie, and we both heard it!"

Of course Merle had to go and investigate. William escorted her at once to the spot. There was a large elm just at the edge of the wood, and certainly it was emitting very strange sounds. At intervals a curious clicking whirr came from among the branches. Mr. and Mrs. Treasure, who had also been informed of the mysterious noises, had hurried up from the farm with little Connie. They stood staring upwards in much perplexity.

"Could it be a bird?" suggested Merle.

"That's no bird! It's something beyond that!" said Mr. Treasure solemnly.

"Oh! Is it an omen? My mother's been ill the last fortnight!" exclaimed Mrs. Treasure in much distress.

"Maybe it's a warning of some kind or another!" opined the postman, who had been passing and had joined the party.

Whatever might occasion the noises, they continued with great regularity. The postman, continuing his round, spread news of the strange happening, and soon quite a number of people came into the wood to listen for themselves. No one was in the least able to account for the sounds, and the general opinion was that the tree was haunted. Superstition ran rife, and most of the neighbours considered it must be a portent. Poor Mrs. Treasure began to be quite sure it had some intimate connection with her mother's illness. Several girls were weeping hysterically, and one of them asked if the end of the world was coming. Meantime, more and more people kept crowding into the wood, and the idea spread that some disaster was imminent.

"My John's out with the trawler!" wailed one woman. "I wish I'd not let him go! As like as not he'll be wrecked!"

"You never know!" agreed a friend.

Old Grandfather Treasure, who had hobbled up from the stackyard, quoted texts from Scripture and began to improve the occasion. His daughter-in-law, with Connie clasped in her arms, sobbed convulsively.

Into the midst of all this excitement suddenly strode Bevis.

"I heard about it down on the quay," he said. "I came up at once. I'll soon show you what it is!"

He was buckling climbing-irons on to his legs while he spoke, and with the aid of these he rapidly mounted the elm tree to where the boughs forked, put his hand into a hollow, and drew out a wooden box, which he brought down with him.

"It's nothing at all ghostly," he explained. "The fact is I'm fearfully keen on photographing birds, and I've just got a cinema camera. There's a sparrow-hawk's nest in the next tree, and I want to take pictures of it; only I knew the clicking of the cinema business would scare them away probably for hours, so I made a little mechanical contrivance that would go on clicking and let them get used to the noise, so that they'd take no notice when I really went to work. You can look at it if you want to."

It was such a simple explanation that those among the neighbours who had most loudly expressed superstitious fears looked rather foolish, and the crowd began to melt away.

"Why didn't you tell us about it, Bevis?" asked Merle in private.

"Well, Soeurette, the fact is the birds are so shy that the fewer people who go and watch them the better for the success of a photograph. I'm afraid this will have sent them off altogether. Annoying, isn't it? Can't be helped, though, now. It's a good dodge all the same, and I shall try it again in some other tree when I can find a nest I want to take. Better luck next time, I hope!"

CHAPTER XV

LEAVE-TAKINGS

The precious delightful holidays at Chagmouth seemed to be flying only too fast. All the various young people were busy with their several hobbies, but they liked to meet and compare notes about them, and took a keen interest in one another's achievements. Bevis's bird-photography, and especially his cinema camera, was highly appreciated, particularly by the younger members of the party, who persistently tried to track him and follow him, greatly to his embarrassment, for their presence frightened the birds away and defeated the very object for which he had gone out. Mavis had struck up a friendship with Miss Lindsay and Lorraine Forrester, and often went to see them at the studio which they had temporarily hired. Lorraine's principal branch of art was sculpture, and she was modelling a bust of Morland, who came readily for sittings, though he had refused point-blank to act model for his father.

The two were on terms of what Lorraine called "sensible friendship," which Mavis suspected might mean a good deal more some day, if Morland stopped merely drifting and put his shoulder in dead earnest to the wheel of life. Lorraine was much the stronger character of the two, and could generally wind up Morland's ambition while he was with her, though it often came down again with a run as soon as her influence was removed. Whether or no her feelings went deeper than she would at present allow, she was a loyal chum to him, and almost the only person who could really persuade him to work.

To Claudia also Lorraine was a splendid friend. The girls lived together at a Students' Hostel in London, and shared all their jaunts and pleasures. Claudia held a scholarship at a college of music, and was training for grand opera. With her talent and lovely face she had good prospects before her, but the Castleton strain was strong in her, as also in Morland, and it needed Lorraine's insistent urging to make her realise that it does not do only to dream your ideals, that you must toil at them with strong hands and earth-stained fingers, and that on this physical plane no success can ever be achieved without hard work.

"They'll both of them absolutely have to be towed through life!" thought Mavis. "I could shake the whole family sometimes. Beata's the most practical, but the others might have strayed out of a poetry book! Of course they're all perfectly charming and romantic, but you want to frame them and glaze them and hang them in exhibitions, not set them to do ordinary every-day things. They don't fit somehow into the twentieth century. Lorraine stirs them up like yeast. She'll be the making of Morland if she elects to take on so big a job."

The Ramsay girls were very much attracted by the Macleods. They liked Fay and her father and mother, whose experience of the world and sensible views appealed to them. They often went to Bella Vista and enjoyed a chat, or sat looking at American art magazines, while Morland, who could not keep away from the grand piano, sat improvising memories of Debussy or compositions of his own. Mrs. Macleod was one of those delightful women who can appreciate other people's daughters as well as their own. Her adoration for Fay did not hinder her from genuinely admiring Mavis and Merle and Romola, and the other young friends who flocked to her hospitable house. She had a nice word for them all, and was so sympathetic that they always wanted to tell her of their little achievements. It was a most congenial atmosphere.

"She's such a *dear*!" commented Mavis. "Now when Fay and I went out painting together, she praised my sketch, although it was a daub compared with Fay's! Once I was silly enough to show one of my efforts to Mrs. Earnshaw; she put on her pince-nez, and looked at it most critically, and said,' Oh, you must see *Opal's* work! She's done some really *beautiful* paintings at Brackenfield! They know how to teach there!' I felt so squashed!"

"Mrs. Earnshaw is the limit!" agreed Merle. "The last time I went to tea there-when you had a cold and couldn't go-she asked me to play the piano. I'd brought my music, but I didn't like to seem too anxious, so I said I'd rather not. 'Oh, never mind then!' she said, 'you play something, darling!' (to Opal). And then she whispered proudly to me, 'Opal plays magnificently since she's been to Brackenfield!' I wanted to sing out 'Cock-a-doodle-doo!' only I remembered my manners. Then a friend came in, and she introduced us. 'This is Miss Ramsay,' she said casually, 'and this (with immense pride) is our daughter Opal!' I felt inclined to quote, 'Look on this picture and on that!' It was so evident which of us he was expected to take notice of! I simply wasn't to be in it at all!"

"Opal's more decent, though, since she's been at Brackenfield."

"There was room for improvement. I shall never like her, not if I know her to all eternity."

The glorious three weeks at Chagmouth were over at last, and there would be no more picnics on the beach, or walks down primrose-decked lanes, or rambles on the cliffs, or merry parties at The Haven or Bella Vista, or expeditions in search of flowers or shells. The girls were almost weeping when it came to saying good-bye to Burswood Farm, and to Mr. and Mrs. Treasure, and William and little Connie, and Ethel the small servant (brought up from the village to wait on the visitors), and Charlie, the boy who helped to milk the cows and weed the fields. Mavis and Merle had been very busy concocting one of their wonderful rhyming effusions, and wrote it in the Visitors' Book, much to the delight of their landlady, who appreciated such souvenirs.

> Who welcomed us to Burswood Farm
> Amid the heart of Devon's charm,
> With skies so blue and seas so calm?
>   'Twas Mrs. Treasure.
>
> Who was it chopped our logs of wood
> To make our fires so bright and good,
> And brought from Durracombe our food?
>   'Twas Mr. Treasure.
>
> Who brought our luggage to the door
> And then went back to fetch some more,
> And showed us cows and pigs galore?
>   'Twas Charlie.
>
> Who made our boots and shoes to shine,
> And brought us plates wherewith to dine,
> And boiled our breakfast eggs by nine?
>   'Twas Ethel.
>
> Who was it gave us ferns so green
> From hedges that we'd often seen,
> And called the holiday a dream?
>   'Twas William.
>
> Who was it down the passage ran
> And shouted, 'Kiss me if you can!'
> And hid her face when we began?
>   'Twas Connie.
>
> Who was it left with many a sigh,
> As to the farm we said good-bye,
> And wanted sheets wherein to cry?
>   We all!

The very best of things, however, must come some time to an end; schools were reopening, college terms recommencing, Mr.

Tremayne's duties claimed him in London, and, most prosaic of all, another batch of visitors was expected at Burswood, so that they could no longer have the rooms. After tremendous leave-takings the jolly party separated, Dr. Ramsay fetching Mavis and Merle in the car, while Mr. and Mrs. Tremayne took Clive home with them, for he was to try another term at his preparatory school. It seemed quite quiet at Bridge House without their lively young cousin, though in some ways his absence was rather a relief. After his many escapades at Chagmouth the girls felt that discipline under a headmaster would be very wholesome for him. They themselves were busy with the work of the coming term, and not sorry to be free from his continual interruption of their preparation time. There were other things besides lessons. They meant to take up tennis very seriously, and practise both on the school courts and at home. Miss Mitchell was a tennis enthusiast and also Miss Barnes.

"If we can only persuade Miss Hopkins and Mademoiselle to do their duty we could have a match 'Mistresses versus Girls,'" sighed Merle. "It would be something new at 'The Moorings,' and such an excitement for every one."

"I wish they would!"

"If I were a boarder I'd simply *make* them! What they want is somebody to keep them up to it. Day-girls are really very much hampered. They haven't half a chance when they go home from school at four o'clock. I really sometimes think I'd like to be a boarder, just for the fun of it."

It is not very often we get what we want, but on this occasion Fortune waved a fairy wand and gave Merle the luck she coveted. It happened that the cook at Bridge House developed a sore throat, and Dr. Ramsay, having his suspicions, had the drains examined and found them to be in an exceedingly wrong condition. It was necessary to take them up at once, and as the process would probably be unpleasant, Mrs. Ramsay arranged for the girls to stay at 'The Moorings' until everything was once more in good sanitary condition.

"You can't be too careful where young people are concerned," was her motto. "Mavis is so marvellously well now that we don't want to run any risks, and Merle, too, strong though she is, will be better out of the way of drains. We elders can take our chance."

To be temporarily transformed into boarders was a novel experience for the girls. To Merle it meant an opportunity for making a much more intimate acquaintance with her idol Miss Mitchell, with whom she would now be at close quarters. To sit at the same table with her for meals seemed an unspeakable privilege. Merle was at the age for enthusiastic hero-worship, and in her eyes the popular mistress almost wore a halo. That she bestowed no particular tokens of favour made the devotion none the less, because it gave an added incentive for trying to win at least a glance or a smile.

Though Merle's schoolgirl affections centred in Miss Mitchell, whose modern, up-to-date, twentieth-century methods and opinions entirely appealed to her, Mavis was glad to see something more of Miss Pollard and Miss Fanny. She had loved 'The Moorings' best as it was a year ago, a little 'homey' school, where the classes had been like working with a private governess. She immensely admired the two sweet, grey-haired sisters, with their refined, cultured atmosphere and beautiful, courteous, dignified manner. They seemed the epitome of the nineteenth century, and marked a different era, a something very precious that was rapidly passing away. If flowers are the symbols of our personalities she would have set them down as rosemary and lavender. They had withdrawn almost entirely from teaching, so that the day-girls now saw little of them, but in the hostel they still reigned supreme, and kept to their old custom of amusing the youngest boarders for half an hour before bedtime. The elder ones, owing to the large amount of preparation required under the new regime, could very rarely find time now to come and join this pleasant circle, which met in quite an informal manner in Miss Pollard's room. To Mavis it was a bigger attraction even than tennis, and she would give up her turn at the courts, or would hurry over her home-work, in order to creep in among the juniors for that cosy half-hour.

"Have you written down any more Devonshire folk-tales?" she asked once. "I do so love your stories of the neighbourhood. It makes the pixies seem almost real when you tell about them!"

"They seemed real to the old people from whom I heard them years ago, and who had learnt them from their grandfathers and great-grandfathers. I loved them when I was a child. Yes; they're written in my little manuscript book. I put them carefully down for fear I might forget them. Read you one? If the others would like it! We haven't had a fairy tale for quite a long time, have we, Doreen?"

As the younger children plumped for a story, Miss Pollard fetched her manuscript volume, and hunted for something they had not yet heard. She was a most excellent reader, having that charm of voice and vividness of expression which makes a narrative live before its hearers. It was as if some electric cord linked her with those who listened, and restless little fidgets would sit quite quietly for as long as she chose to go on. The tale which she selected to-night was:

GINNIFER'S DOWRY

In the days when good King Arthur ruled all the west country from Exeter to Land's End, a maiden named Ginnifer lived with her father in a little, round, stone hut on the top of Dartmoor. They were poor, but she was a good girl, and she could spin, and weave baskets, and do many things about the house. One day a young hunter knocked at the door and asked for hospitality, and as there was much game to be had in the neighbourhood he remained for many weeks as a guest of the cottage, going out every day fishing or fowling, and sharing his captures with his hosts. No doubt Ginnifer's blue eyes and gentle glances were the main attraction, and in a short time indeed the young folk became attached to one another. It was only when Ginnifer's father at length questioned the youth, that he confessed to being the son of the great lord of the neighbourhood, who lived in the big Castle beside the river beyond the moor. This was sad news for Ginnifer, for in those days a young noble might not wed with a poor girl, and must marry a bride who could bring a rich dowry with her of jewels and ornaments and silver money. So she quietly told her sweetheart to go back to his father, and learn to forget her; and he went away very sadly, vowing he would get permission to return and marry her, or else he would never wed anyone. When he was gone, Ginnifer went out over the moor among the heather, where she might fight her grief alone, with only the birds and the flowers to see her weep. She lay on the short moorland grass among the sweet bog-myrtle and asphodel, until the sun was setting in a red ball over the hillside. Then, all of a sudden, she heard a rustling and a whispering like countless leaves blown by an autumn wind.

"Who is this?" said a voice. "Who dares to lie in our pixie ring?"

"It's a mortal! A mortal!" cried another.

Ginnifer raised her head. All the moor was alive with tiny pixies, whose green garments were like moving fronds of fern. They crowded eagerly round her.

"It's Ginnifer!" they said. "Ginnifer who lives in the stone hut on the moor! Ginnifer who tended the plover with the broken wing, and watered the harebells that were withering in the burning sun, and who treads so lightly that the birds don't trouble to fly away from her. We know her kindness and her gentle heart, for the 'good folk' watch over the children of the earth, and, unseen, we have followed her through all her simple life. Pretty Ginnifer, tell us your trouble. The pixies cannot bear to see you weep."

They stroked her hair with their tiny fingers, they bathed her eyes with dewdrops and wiped them with the petals of a wild

Angela Brazil

rose. At first Ginnifer was frightened, but the little folk were so kind that she took courage and told them her trouble. They began to dance and jump about with delight, and clapped their little hands.

"Is that all?" they shouted. "Would he wed you if you were a great lady? Tell us what dowry his father would expect his bride to bring?"

"Silks and jewels!" sobbed poor Ginnifer, "and rich embroidered dresses, and trinkets of gold, and caskets of silver money! And I have nothing at all!"

The pixies laughed lustily, throwing up their wee green caps into the air and catching them again for sheer joy.

"Ginnifer dear! We'll find you your dowry! Quick! Let us set to work! We must finish our task before daybreak."

By this time the moon had risen and had flooded the moor with light. Like a flight of busy buzzing bees the little people went flitting up and down. They pulled the gossamer from the gorse bushes and wove it into the finest silk; they caught the great brown moths and sheared their soft fur and spun it on the daintiest little spinning-wheels in the world; and with skilful touches they wove together the harebells and the wild rose petals into the most wonderful of embroidered gowns. The tears which Ginnifer had shed in her sorrow lay shining among the grass, and gathered up by magic fingers they turned into pearls and diamonds fit for a queen. The gorse flowers became golden ornaments, and the little smooth pebbles in the brook changed into pieces of silver money.

The pixies dressed Ginnifer in the softest of the gossamer silk robes, they clasped the golden bracelets round her arms and twisted diamonds into her hair.

"Now she is a fairy princess," they said. "There is none lovelier in all Elfland. We must build her a palace worthy of her!"

Hither and thither they ran, gathering up the dewdrops, and piling them one above the other till the most wonderful Castle rose up on the hillside: as clear as glass, it shone with all the colours of the rainbow, and here they stored the silks and the beautiful ornaments and the caskets of silver money.

Next morning Ginnifer's lover came riding back to tell her that his father forbade the match, but that he meant to marry her whether or no. And lo and behold! he found her at the door of a pixie palace, and directly he set foot inside it, it sank through the ground and carried them both with it into Elfland. And there they have lived ever since, as happy as the pixies themselves, though no one on earth saw them any more. But sometimes when the late sickle moon shines over the moor, travellers who have lost their way have been set in the right path by a lovely lady in gauzy green garments, who sprang up, as it seemed, from nowhere, and vanished away again into the mist, and to this day the children, hunting for bilberries on the hillside, call the shining dewdrops 'Ginnifer's tears.'"

"Have you ever seen any pixies yourself, Miss Pollard?" asked Doreen eagerly.

"No; but I've seen the dewdrops shining just like diamonds, and I've seen the mist make wonderful pixie castles in the moonlight. We can live in a fairy world of our own if we look at the right things. It depends on your eyes. Those people who keep their childhood have the pixies all round them."

"You have!" said Mavis, as Miss Pollard rose to say good-night to her circle of listeners. "You're like Peter Pan, and never grow old!"

"I had such a happy childhood! And it seemed so much the best part of life that I've always been reluctant to let the glamour go. Children ought to be brought up on fairy tales! They're incipient poetry, and should be woven into the web of our lives as a beautiful border, before all the dark prose part follows. If the shuttle only weaves matter-of-fact threads it spoils the pattern!"

CHAPTER XVI

THE TADPOLE CLUB

It was quite interesting to be a boarder at 'The Moorings,' though it had its more sober side, particularly for Merle. Her trouble lay in the fact that though she was a school officer from 9 A.M. to 4 P.M., out of those hours her authority was non-existent. Iva and Nesta were hostel monitresses, and they had quite plainly and firmly given her to understand that they did not expect any interference. They were perfectly within their rights, and Merle knew it, but she chafed nevertheless. The fact was that Iva and Nesta, accustomed to the old traditions of 'The Moorings,' when there were only about a dozen boarders, were quite unable to cope with the new order of things, and girls who had been to other schools took decided advantage of their slackness. Merle, whose motto was 'once a monitress always a monitress,' could not see why she might reprove Norma Bradley in the playground, but must allow that damsel ostentatiously to do exactly the same act in the recreation room under her very nose.

"It's so bad for the kids!" she raged. "They know Iva and Nesta are weak and just pretend not to notice, so as to have no fuss. I'm sure Miss Mitchell can't know all that goes on or she'd make some different arrangement. You feel in another element when you get into the hostel. It's 'do as you like and don't bother me so long as you don't go too far and aren't found out.' It might be all very well in the old days last year, but it's wrecking the show now. I wouldn't have believed it if I didn't

Angela Brazil

see it with my own eyes."

The chief offenders were three Third form girls, Norma Bradley, Biddy Adams, and Daisy Donovan, who, with those former firebrands Winnie Osborne and Joyce Colman, had formed a kind of Cabal, whose object seemed to be to find out how far rules might be evaded.

"They've more time than we have, and they simply 'rag' about and 'play the giddy goat'!" complained Merle to her sister.

"They don't seem to have enough to do with their spare time," commented Mavis. "It's all very well to say they must have absolute recreation, but both they and the babies turn it into a sort of bear-garden. You were rather a terror yourself when you were that age! I remember Mother used to quote, 'Satan finds some mischief still for idle hands'."

"Was I? And now I'm a monitress!"

"It makes all the difference when you're in authority, and have some stake in the school."

This chance remark set Merle thinking, and she thought to some purpose. Her natural disposition was always to obtain results by blunt, matter-of-fact methods. In school her policy was, 'Come along with you now, I'm not going to have any nonsense!' Backed by her position, her strong personality, and her prowess at games it succeeded. But here in the hostel, if she wished to effect any improvements, she must go about it another way. The old fable of the wind and the sun would apply, school breezes would be useless, and she must switch on the love-radiator and try smiling.

"I believe I *was* rather a terror at twelve," she acknowledged to herself. "It's such a tiresome age; you're no longer a pet lamb, and yet you're not a senior. You get all the snubs and none of the kisses. I used to long to do a little bossing on my own, instead of trailing like a comet's tail after the big girls. What those kids want is a properly organised club. They'd work the steam off in that. I've a very good mind to draw up a scheme, show it to Miss Mitchell, and ask her if I may start it among the juniors. If I have her leave, then Iva and Nesta can't call it interfering."

It took Merle a little trouble to evolve her idea, but with a remembrance of Girl Guiding she decided on forming a company corresponding to the Brownies, the objects of which should be to train its members to win various school honours. It was to have its own officers, and its own committees, and to concentrate upon cricket practice, badminton, and net-ball, as well as First Aid, knot-tying, and signalling.

Feeling rather nervous and a little uncertain whether she would meet with approval or a rebuff, she carried her scheme to Miss Mitchell's study. The mistress listened quite composedly and thought for a moment or two.

"You may try it, Merle, if you can persuade the children to join," she said at length. "You have my full sanction, and you may tell them so. We'll see how it succeeds."

It was something to have leave from headquarters. Merle hurried away and lost no time in collecting the junior boarders, who came to her meeting out of sheer curiosity to see what she could possibly want with them. For once blunt plain-spoken Merle was silver-tongued, and advocated her club with all the ingenuity of which she was capable.

"A school is no good if it depends entirely on its elder girls," she said artfully. "In a year or two they'll have left, and it's the middle forms who'll be at the top. If those middle forms will only begin and train themselves *now*, they'll be champions by the time they reach the Sixth, and there'd be some sense in making fixtures for tennis and cricket. It generally takes a school years before it begins to win matches. Why? Because it must train its champions, of course. You" (nodding at the Cabal) "are the sort who ought to win cups and shields for

'The Moorings' in another four years or so. And it's your business to teach the younger ones. I saw Doreen and Elsbeth playing cricket with Joyce to-day in a way that absolutely made me shudder. She should show them how to hold their bats, and never allow leg-before-wicket even with the veriest kid. It's no use letting them start bad habits, is it? My suggestion is that you form yourselves into a club; let the elder ones be officers, and give efficiency badges for certain things. You've so much more time than we seniors have, that you ought to get on like a house on fire. You'd be laying the foundations of some very good work later on. I should call you the 'Pioneers,' because you'd be starting on a new venture to spread the fame of 'The Moorings.' What d'you think about it?"

The idea decidedly appealed to the juniors. It was far more flattering to be told they were the coming strength of the school than that they were nuisances and in the way of the older girls. Moreover, the notion of being officers was attractive to such temperaments as Winnie's, Biddy's, and Daisy's. They thought they should rather enjoy training the younger ones, and giving their opinions at committee meetings. It was so dull simply to form audiences while the seniors did the talking.

"I vote we do!" said Winnie, looking at the rest of the Cabal, who nodded approvingly in reply.

"Very well. You must organise your own committees, but I think every now and then there should be an inspection to show how you're getting on. You can choose any one you like for your commissioner. A teacher if you want."

"Might as well have you as anybody!" murmured Winnie.

"You can decide that later. What I advise you to do is to hold a committee among yourselves, write down your officers and your rules and everything, and then set to work."

The plan answered admirably, from the mere fact that it gave the restless juniors something definite to do in their recreation time. Instead of tearing aimlessly about and getting into mischief, they suddenly became the most busy little mortals, and absolutely bristled with importance. Their committees were conducted with as much solemnity as the meetings of Cabinet ministers to decide the fate of a nation. They had taken the burden of the future success of the school upon their youthful shoulders, and it gave them huge satisfaction to think that so much depended upon them. They practised cricket quite diligently, and made even the youngest observe the rules, and they bandaged one another's arms and legs in well-meant efforts at ambulance work. Their ambition soared as high as a debating society, where they evidently allowed full freedom of speech on popular topics, for Mavis, by mistake getting hold of one of their secret notices, found the subject for discussion was: "*Monnitresses. Are they a Neccessary Evil?*"

She showed it to Merle with much amusement.

"I should suggest, 'Need Spelling copy the Dictionary?' for their next debate!" she laughed. "I wish I could creep in, Merle, and hear them slanging you four. I expect they'll give you some hard hits. How priceless they are!"

With the exception of Mavis the elder girls were not entirely in sympathy with the new movement. They considered the Pioneers exhibited signs of swollen head, and nicknamed their society the 'Tadpole Club,' declaring its members to be still in that elementary stage of their development. They made very merry at their expense, and poked fun at Merle for having evolved the idea.

"Have you arranged for the Queen to come down and inspect them?" asked Nesta sarcastically. "No one but royalty is good enough! By the time they've worked their way up into the Sixth the school will be so reformed it'll be a pattern for all England. I think we seniors had better retire gracefully now and have done with it. We don't seem of much account according to their notions. One of them actually had the impudence to criticise my bowling yesterday!"

"Yes; and the little beggar was right too!" put in Iva. "You'll have to buck up over cricket, old sport! It never was your strong point, you know!"

"Well, I'm not going to be corrected by a kid of eleven at any rate!" fumed Nesta.

Though the seniors might be scornful, indignant, or otherwise hostile towards the Tadpole Club, it certainly had the effect of increasing their own efforts and making them keep up their standards. A craze came over the school for physical fitness and efficiency, and the most persistent shirkers were forced by public opinion into exerting themselves. Miss Mitchell said little, but her hazel eyes saw everything that was going on. Her manner towards Merle, which had been rather off-hand, gradually softened, and though she showed her no special favour, she gave her, on one occasion, a word of praise.

"You've shown me that you possess certain powers of organisation, and that you know how to use your influence," she remarked.

And Merle, to whom Miss Mitchell's good opinion seemed almost the most important thing in the world, went about as if she were treading on air, and repeated the precious sentence to herself as proudly as if it were a patent of nobility.

"She wouldn't notice me when I used to bring her flowers!" thought Merle. "It's only when I've done something for the school that she really cares. Some day, perhaps, I'll make her like me for myself!"

CHAPTER XVII

THE FOURTH OF JULY

Mavis and Merle went home to Bridge House feeling as if they had had a peep at the inner life of 'The Moorings.' They had seen fresh aspects of Miss Pollard and Miss Fanny, and though Merle could not honestly assure herself that she knew Miss Mitchell any better than before, she had at least the remembrance of a few words of approval.

"I'm afraid she's one of those people whom you never do get to know very well!" ruminated Merle. "You go a little way, but never any further. We see the school side of her, and a quite jolly-all-round-to-everybody holiday afternoon side. I wonder what she's like to her private friends, and at home?"

Miss Mitchell, however, was not at all disposed to make a confidante of any of her pupils, particularly of a girl who was not yet sixteen, and much preferred to preserve business-like relations and confine her conversation to school topics, than to give any details of her private life. She made it quite manifest that whoever wished to please her must do so on general and not individual grounds, so Merle accepted the inevitable, and worked very hard in class and at preparation, making a sudden burst of progress in her lessons that astonished herself even more than everybody else. It meant a certain amount of heroism to stick steadily to her books on glorious summer evenings, when even her own family tempted her to play tennis or go out in the car. Most of the other members of the Fifth

Angela Brazil

form showed a marked slacking off in their homework, particularly the day-girls, whose preparation was not regulated. The Castletons, who had another wee baby brother at home, declared they found so much to do on their return that it was impossible to spend long over their lessons.

"Violet's not very strong, and she's often just about done in when we get back," explained Beata to Mavis. "Romola and I take the baby and put the kids to bed, so as to give her a rest. I can't tell that to Miss Mitchell as an excuse for not having touched my Latin, but it's the truth. What else can I do? We've only one maid, and she's busy in the kitchen. Somebody has to look after the children!"

And Mavis, who adored the new Castleton baby, and would have flung lessons to the winds to nurse it, cordially agreed with her.

Another girl whose work suffered in summer, though for a different reason, was Fay. Her father was better in health, but he still needed somebody to interest him and keep him amused, and found no more lively companion than his own daughter. He had taught her to row, and wanted her to go out boating with him now the evenings were so long and light.

"Never mind your prep! It's more important to help to get Father well!" Mrs. Macleod would say. "He looks forward so much to this rowing, and the exercise is good for him. We want a companionable daughter, not a Minerva, and you may tell Miss Mitchell so with my compliments if she grumbles. If we can't have any of your society when you get home, you might as well be away at boarding-school. I bargained with Miss Pollard that you weren't to be overworked."

Fay was clever, and a hasty run through her books usually served to make her pass muster in class. She was a jolly and amusing girl, and was generally the life and soul of the 'sardine' party. She was great chums with the Castletons, though she sparred occasionally with Tattie Carew or with Nan Colville.

The latter gave general offence because she always insisted upon taking up more than her fair share of room in the crowded car. She would wear her satchel, and let its knobby corners press against her expostulating neighbour, or she would spread out her elbows instead of keeping them by her side. One day Nan, after a scrimmage on the way to school, begged a lift back from Babbie.

"But we don't go down the hill to Chagmouth," objected Babbie, who had received instructions from her mother to allow the 'sardines' to use their own car, and not to offer to motor any of them. "We turn off at the cross-roads to go to The Warren."

"I know. But you always start first, and you could leave me at the cross-roads, and the others would pick me up as they passed. Be a sport, Babbie!"

"All right. You can come if you like."

Now it happened that Fay overheard Nan telling Lizzie that she would wait at the cross-roads, and further witnessed the magnificent start in the Glyn Williams' car.

"Too good for us to-day, are you?" she murmured. "Then I think you may just do without us altogether! I've got a brain throb! It'll serve you right, Miss Nan Colville!"

Fay went privately to Mr. Vicary and asked him if he would mind driving them home that afternoon by Brendon, which was a slightly different route from their ordinary one.

"I want to call for a parcel there," she explained.

"As it happens, I have an errand I can do there too," agreed Mr. Vicary. "It won't take above five minutes or so longer, I daresay."

"That's all right then. By the by, Miss Colville won't be with

Angela Brazil

us to-day. Miss Williams is motoring her home."

"Yes; I saw them set off."

Fay took care that Lizzie Colville sat at the back of the car that afternoon and not in front with Mr. Vicary. She stifled her objections when they turned off in the direction of Brendon.

"I tell you Mr. Vicary has to go on an errand and so have I, so just shut up! Nan? If she chooses to wait at the cross-roads it's her own fault. She should have come with us."

The 'sardine-tin' entered Chagmouth that afternoon from the direction of Brendon, and Nan, after sitting a long time by the roadside expecting its appearance, gave it up and walked the rest of the way home, very annoyed at the trick that had been played her.

"You shouldn't have let them, Lizzie!" she scolded.

"How could I help it? Fay wouldn't let me speak, and Mr. Vicary just flew on to Brendon. Why didn't Babbie take you into Chagmouth?"

"She never even suggested it. I don't know which is the meaner, she or Fay!" grumbled Nan.

On the Fourth of July, Fay went to school determined to have what she termed 'a real good time,' and to celebrate appropriately the great anniversary of American independence. She armed herself with her national flag and a box of sugared popcorns, a delicacy which was unknown at Durracombe shops, and had been specially sent for from London. As she passed these round generously, the 'sardines' fell in with her mood and vowed to stand by her at school, and help to celebrate the honour and glory of the Stars and Stripes.

"I didn't make much fuss of my own birthday, but I'm wrought up over this!" declared Fay. "It's a shame there isn't a public holiday. I'd like to fire a cannon. Couldn't get any crackers at those wretched shops in Chagmouth either."

"D'you want crackers?"

"Rather!"

"They had a lot of fireworks last November at Hodges' in Durracombe. Perhaps they'd have some left."

"Oh, good bizz! We'll stop in the High Street and see, before we go into school."

They were in excellent time, so they called a halt at Hodges' shop and dismissed the car. The assistant, after searching in various drawers and boxes, produced a small supply of surplus fireworks, which Fay eagerly purchased, being also provident enough to remember to buy a box of matches. She pranced into school in the highest of spirits, flaunting her flag, and stuck it in a conspicuous place in the classroom, where Miss Mitchell eyed it indeed with some astonishment, but offered no remonstrance. At eleven o'clock interval the fun began. Fay and her confederates retired to a secluded part of the garden and began to let off squibs and crackers, the sound therefrom drawing an interested and excited little crowd, who hopped about squealing at the explosions, and were immensely thrilled at the audacity of such a performance on school premises.

"They're great!"

"Hold me down, or I'll fly off in sparks!"

"Fay, you are the limit!"

"It's a brainy notion!"

"Wow! Don't set me on fire!"

"Goody! Here's Miss Fanny coming!"

Angela Brazil

It was a decidedly wrathful Miss Fanny who descended upon them, and promptly confiscated the few fireworks that were left.

"Most dangerous!" she remarked indignantly. "You might easily, some of you, have been burnt. Really, Fay, I'm surprised. A girl in the Fifth form ought to know better. Go back all of you at once. And don't let such a thing ever happen again!"

The confederates had been lucky enough to have almost finished their display before Miss Fanny appeared on the scene, so they bore the loss of the last three squibs with equanimity.

"If Miss Fanny had only been an American she'd have helped to let them off herself instead of interfering!" protested Fay. "I haven't worked my spirits off yet, so I warn you! We'll do something mad after dinner."

"What?"

"I haven't quite fixed it up yet, but I'll tell you later on."

The girls from Chagmouth dined daily with the boarders in the hostel, and were on very good terms with most of them. Fay could therefore be tolerably sure of a certain amount of support in any scheme she chose to evolve. She thought things over during the French class, a process of mental abstraction which brought the wrath of Mademoiselle on to her head, for she answered at random and made some really idiotic mistakes, at which the other girls giggled.

"You didn't shine this morning, old sport!" whispered Beata when the class was over. "I believe Mademoiselle thought you were ragging her!"

"I wasn't doing anything of the sort. Can't you all realise it's the Fourth of July?"

"You've mentioned that once or twice before!"

"Well, I'll mention it again. Of course I focus my mind on America, not on France! You can't expect me to go jabbering French when I think of the times my friends will be having to-day on the other side of the Atlantic. I've had rather a brain throb though. We'll dress up after dinner in anything we can borrow, and have a parade on the tennis lawn, with prizes for best costumes."

"Who's to give the prizes?"

"*I* will. I'll ask Maude to buy me some packets of candy when she goes home, and bring them to school this afternoon. They'll do all right."

Fay was discreet enough not to mention her project to Iva or Nesta, in case, being hostel monitresses, they might have felt bound to offer conscientious objections. Members of the Fourth and Third forms, however, jumped at the idea of an impromptu fancy-dress parade, and the moment they were released from the dining-room they tore off to array them-selves. It was already a quarter to two, and school would begin again at 2.30, so there was no time to be lost if the thing was to be done at all.

"I give every one a quarter of an hour to dress!" declared Fay. "You've got to be on the lawn when the clock strikes two. Anybody who's late will be disqualified from the competition."

"Who's to judge?" asked Kitty.

"Votes, of course! Don't stand asking questions. Hurry up, if you're going to be in it!"

A quarter of an hour is very scant time in which to robe in fancy costume, but most of the girls had decided during dinner what they meant to be. Romola flew to the kitchen and borrowed an apron from the cook, tied a duster round her head, seized up a pail and a carpet-sweeper, and came as 'Domestic Service.' Beata commandeered the boarders' bath-towels and appeared as an Arab, in robe and turban. Peggie, with her dormitory eider-down for a train, was a court lady. Catie draped a scarf over her hair and shoulders and, holding a bedroom jug aloft on her head, posed as Rebecca at the well. Nan and Tattie, wrapt in identical blankets, were Tweedledum and Tweedledee. Winnie, with a painted moustache and a dressing-gown, was a Turk. Nita slipped on a night-dress and clutched a bedroom candlestick; Joyce rolled an enormous brown-paper cigar which she pretended to be puffing. But perhaps the best of all was Fay herself as the American eagle. She borrowed two mackintoshes and fastened them to her shoulders, securing the other ends to blackboard pointers which she held in each hand. By extending her arms at full width she gave the impression of wings and flapped wildly round the lawn, the illusion being furthered by a brown-paper head-dress with a long twist to resemble a beak.

When the day-girls returned after dinner they were electrified to find this extraordinary assemblage parading upon the lawn. By this time both monitresses and mistresses had caught glimpses from the window and came hurrying out to see what was happening. Fortunately Miss Mitchell, who arrived first on the scene, took it in what the girls called 'a thoroughly sporting fashion.' She laughed, and congratulated the wearers upon the excellence of their hasty costumes.

"We must have another parade some day, when we've more time to prepare for it," she said. "Perhaps I'll come in costume myself then. The American eagle is simply immense! I give Fay my vote for first prize! Hands up all who agree!"

"But *I'm* giving the prize, so I can't take it myself!" protested Fay.

"That doesn't matter at all if you've won it. I think Tweedledum and Tweedledee should divide the second."

"Best divide the candy all round," said Fay, receiving the packets from Maude, and sharing them among the competitors. "Thanks awfully, Miss Mitchell, for coming to look at us. I couldn't let the Fourth of July go by without taking some notice of it! It wouldn't have been loyal to America, would it?"

"You've certainly stood up for the honour of the Stars and Stripes!" laughed Miss Mitchell. "Now suppose you all go and take these things off again as fast as you can. My watch is exactly right, and the bell will ring in another five minutes."

Angela Brazil

CHAPTER XVIII

LOVE-IN-A-MIST

The next event of any special importance in the Ramsays' world was Mavis's birthday. She was seventeen now, and was so much taller and stronger since she had come to live in Devonshire that her mother declared their old friends in the north would hardly know her. She was still more fragile-looking than Merle, but her attacks of bronchitis were luckily things of the past, and she was rapidly outgrowing all her former delicacy. Many things which had been prohibited before were allowed her now, and her father's present was a new bicycle and the permission to ride it. Her mother gave her a sketching easel and Merle a camp-stool, for painting was at present her favourite hobby, and Uncle David and Aunt Nellie were lavish in books and music. From Bevis arrived a wooden box containing a kittiwake, which he had stuffed himself, with wings outspread. There was a hook in its back so that it could be suspended by a piece of thread from the ceiling to look as if it were flying. In its beak Bevis had placed a note.

"I didn't shoot it," he explained. "I know you hate to think of any one killing them. I found it dead on the shore, so thought you might just as well have it stuffed."

"I'm so glad it wasn't shot on purpose, poor dear thing!" said tender-hearted Mavis. "Aren't its feathers soft and lovely? I shall hang it to the beam in our bedroom, and it will always seem like a little bit of Chagmouth when we wake in the mornings. It looks just exactly as if it were alive. How clever of Bevis to stuff it so well."

At 'The Moorings' the matter of most vital interest was the arrival of a large wooden hut, which Miss Pollard had bought from the Government, and which was erected in a corner of the garden close to the house. Now that numbers had increased so much in the school extra accommodation was urgently needed, and the new building would serve for a gymnasium, and as a room for lectures and meetings. The great matter for speculation was whether it would be finished in time for term-end festivities. Miss Pollard, urged on by Miss Mitchell, contemplated inviting parents and friends to a formal Speech Day, an affair upon which she had never ventured before. Unless the hut was ready it would be impossible to accommodate so many people, so she hurried on the work and hoped for the best. It was a great amusement to her pupils to watch the various parts being fitted together, and to see the corrugated iron roof fastened on. They rejoiced immensely when at last a flag floated from the top.

"Mr. Perkins says he can undertake to have all perfectly ready by the 25th. I can send out my invitations now!" purred Miss Pollard.

Before Speech Day, however, must come the inevitable examinations. Everybody felt they were much more wearing in July than at Christmas or Easter, owing to the heat, and also to the fact that they covered the work of the whole school year, and not merely that of a single term. Mavis did her utmost but had to struggle with bad headaches, and realised that she had not done herself justice. Merle slogged away grimly, with ink-stained fingers and her hair tied tightly back because of the heat. She had never really taken so much pains over an examination before, and had never found herself so well prepared. Quite to her surprise her brains felt clear and collected, and her mental car seemed to whizz along so fast it quite exceeded the speed limit. No other girl in the form wrote so many sheets as she did or answered such a large proportion of the questions. At the end of the week, tired, nervy, and decidedly cross, she nevertheless felt some satisfaction over the papers she had sent in. Every one in the Fifth had little doubt about the results, and public opinion was justified, for Merle came out top in almost every subject, gaining an average of 91 per cent on the whole exam. She had expected to do well, but was quite staggered at this success, for Muriel, Iva, and Nesta, her usual rivals, were left far and away behind. They were sporting enough to give her their congratulations.

"It means first prize, old thing! Won't we give you a clap as you march on to the platform!" said Iva.

Miss Pollard was determined to do this, her first Speech Day, in style; the chair was to be taken by a local magnate, and the prizes distributed by a real live professor from Oxford, who was spending his vacation in the neighbourhood. There was a tremendous business moving forms and chairs into the newly-erected hut, and decorating the platform with pots of plants and ferns. All the pupils were dressed in white and wore their best hair ribbons. Mavis was feeling sad and sentimental, for it was her last term. She was to leave 'The Moorings' and concentrate her energies on music, and on lessons in painting from Mr. Castleton, which would suit her far better than the strenuous work of the Sixth form. To the girls, and especially the younger ones, this first public function at school was not altogether unmixed bliss. They were obliged to sit as quiet as rows of little angels, packed tightly together on forms without backs, and to listen to interminable speeches about subjects which they only half understood, the main points of which seemed to be, however, that Miss Pollard and Miss Fanny and Miss Mitchell and all the teachers and all the pupils were much to be congratulated, and everybody must remember that 'Rome was not built in a day.'

"Nor the hut either!" whispered Winnie to her chum, applying the proverb too literally. "I wish they'd seen it before the roof was on!"

"'How the creatures talk!'" quoted Joyce, from *Alice in Wonderland*. "I'm bored to tears!"

The prize-giving part was more interesting. As the names were called, each winner in turn walked up to the platform, received her book, bowed more or less gracefully, and retired. The applause was a welcome relief to the rank and file, who were tired of sitting at such exemplary attention. It was over at last, and the visitors went to be shown round the school and to be regaled with tea in the dining-room. Professor Hartley, in cap and gown, had crossed the garden to the hostel, and the pupils, some of them suffering from pins and needles, were free to disperse. It was the breaking-up for the day-girls, and to-morrow morning the boarders would be sent home.

"Just a word with you, Merle!" said Miss Mitchell, calling the latter into the study by herself. "I want to tell you that I'm pleased with your work. You've made an effort and shown me what you can do. Next term we shall have a Sixth form, and Miss Pollard agrees with me that it will be advisable to appoint a head girl. That position will fall to you, not only because you're top in the exams, but because we think you have fitted yourself to take it. A head girl is no use unless she can lead; I've been watching you all the year, and you've shown me lately that you understand what is expected. The school is still in an elementary stage, but it has improved immensely, and next year I trust you to do your very best for it."

"Oh, thank you, Miss Mitchell!" gasped Merle, almost too overwhelmed for words.

To be thus chosen out and selected by her idol was a most happy ending to the term, and offered golden opportunities in the coming September. It meant more to her even than her prize. She went at once to tell the good news to her sister.

"I don't like to cackle too loudly, because of Muriel and Nesta," said Mavis. "But I am proud of you! It's been worth the grind, hasn't it?"

"Rather! Though I'm yearning for the holidays. Shall we go to Chagmouth on Saturday?"

"Oh, yes! Bevis breaks up to-morrow, and I expect he'll be at Grimbal's Farm by then. It's his last term at school as well as mine. I wonder how he feels about leaving? I promised, too, to call and see the Castletons."

When the girls reached home, there was a letter on the table for Mavis in Clive's handwriting. They heard from the boy every now and then, though he was not a particularly good correspondent. This epistle, which had apparently been penned on Sunday, was mostly a summary of cricket and anticipations of his holidays. It ended:

Your affec'ate coz, CLIVE.

P.S. - Meant to send you this snap before. Isn't it priceless?

The sting of a scorpion is in its tail. Mavis stooped down and picked up the little photo which had fallen from the envelope on to the floor. Clive had used his Brownie camera at Chagmouth and had promised to post them the results, but had forgotten. This solitary print represented Bevis - there was no mistaking Bevis - but Mavis bent over it with puzzled eyes, for clasped tightly in his arms with her head laid upon his shoulder was a girl. Merle, who snatched the photo away to look at it, decided her identity at once.

"Why, it's Romola! That's the artistic blue dress that Violet made for her!"

"So it is! Where's her plait, though?"

"Hidden behind her, I suppose. I say! They're coming it rather strong, aren't they?"

"Yes. I shouldn't have thought that of Bevis!"

"No more should I!" (Merle was looking annoyed.) "I'd no idea he could be so silly. I shall rag him about this, you bet!"

"I wouldn't!" (Mavis's voice was very quiet.) "Romola is so pretty! Perhaps he *likes* her!"

"Well, it's the first I've seen of it. He's a sly-boots if he does. Somehow it doesn't seem to fit in with Bevis. I'm cross with him. When did Clive take this amazing snap? I wonder he didn't send it on to us before. I think it's not worth keeping, if you ask me!" and Merle, tearing the photo into bits, tossed it into the waste-paper basket.

"Bevis is *our* friend - not the Castletons'!" she added, stumping away most decidedly cross, "and if he's going in for rubbish like this with Romola, he shan't call *me* Soeurette again! He needn't think it. I'll *not* be a sister to Romola! I declare I won't! The sneak!"

But these latter sentiments were muttered to herself, and she took good care that Mavis should not overhear them.

On Saturday morning Merle had a bilious headache, took some breakfast in bed, and announced that she should spend the day lying in the garden. Mavis also began to make excuses for not going to Chagmouth, but Dr. Tremayne pinched her cheek, declared she looked pale, and that the drive would do her good.

"I can't be left without either of my nice little companions!" he complained. "I've got used to having you with me. Besides, Bevis is coming back to-day!"

"I daresay we shall see him next week some time," remarked Mavis demurely. "There's no violent hurry about it."

"Why, no; only -"

"Nonsense, Mavis! Go with your uncle!" broke in Mrs.

Ramsay. "This is the first time I ever remember you wanting to stay away from your beloved Chagmouth. What's the matter with you to-day? Don't be silly! Put on your hat and do as you're wanted. I think these exams have thoroughly tired out both of you. You'll feel better after a little air in the car."

Mother's decisions were always final, so Mavis raised no more objections, particularly as Uncle David was looking the least trifle hurt, and he was such a dear that she wouldn't disappoint him for worlds. He had several visits to pay that morning at houses on the way, so it was later than usual when they arrived at Grimbal's Farm. Fortunately there were few patients waiting, and when these were disposed of, Mrs. Penruddock brought in lunch.

"Bevis not come yet?" inquired Uncle David as he lifted the dish-cover.

"No, indeed, Doctor, and I'm anxious about him! His yacht's been at Port Sennen, having some repairs done, and he arranged to go there straight from school early this morning, and sail her round to Chagmouth."

"Well! The lad can handle a yacht all right."

"It isn't that! Bevis knows as much about sailing as most folks. But there's a nasty sea fog come on, and just as it happens the clapper is gone out of the bell by St. Morval's Head. Bevis is always a terrible one for hugging the coast, and I'm afraid if he doesn't hear the bell he won't quite know where he is in the fog, and he may be on the rocks before he knows they're there. I'd have told him it was gone, but there was no time. I only got his letter this morning. Who'd have expected a fog like this either?"

Mrs. Penruddock's apple face looked quite miserable, but sounds of thumping at the back door drew her away from the parlour, and stopped any further confidences. Mavis ate her lunch thoughtfully.

"Is a fog worse on the sea than on land?" she asked at last.

"It is, if you can't tell where you're going. Who's been fooling with the bell at St. Morval's, I wonder? If the clapper has fallen out, they should have had it put in again at once. But that's just the way with them. It's nobody's business, and everybody puts it on to somebody else until there's an accident. I've no patience with them!"

When the meal was over, Mavis went out to take a peep at the sea, or rather where the sea ought to be, for there was nothing to look at but a white wall of mist, long wreaths of which were blowing inland and trailing like ghosts into the town. She came hurrying back very quickly to Grimbal's Farm, and sought the kitchen.

"Mrs. Penruddock, please, may I borrow your big dinner-bell?" she asked.

"Why, yes, my dear! But whatever do you want that for?"

"I'm going to take it to St. Morval's Head and ring it!"

"Bless you! Not a bad idea either! There'd be no harm done anyhow. I'd go with you if I'd the time. Mind your way along that slippery cliff. Pity your sister's not here to-day!"

"I shall be all right, thanks! The fog isn't so bad on land. It's quite easy to see where one's going."

Grasping the big brass dinner-bell, Mavis set forth, and going by a path above the farm, got out on to the cliffs. She knew the way very well, for she had often been before, and had not the slightest fear of getting lost, even if the mist should grow thicker. She walked briskly along, the track in front of her looking quite plain for several yards, though the sea below was completely hidden. She recognised many familiar points en route, the bank where the spleenwort grew, the ruined shed, a supposed relic of smuggling days, the barbed-wire fence, the

Angela Brazil

group of elder trees, and the blackberry bank. When she came to the slanting gorse bushes which overhung the path, she knew she had reached the beginning of St. Morval's Head, and that she must be just about over the spot where the buoy was floating with its clapperless bell.

"It's the story of the Inchcape rock all over again," she muttered, and sitting down on the bracken she began ringing.

It was monotonous work and tiring too. It made her arm ache, and she had to use her left hand for a while instead. She went on persistently, however, for who knew what little yacht might be venturing near the treacherous rocks below. It was an extraordinarily lonely feeling to be there on the cliff by herself, with the white mist round her, as if she were in the midst of the clouds. She would have been chilly only the exercise kept her warm. She was obliged to rest every now and then, but not for long. She did not mean to give in for some time yet. She kept repeating over and over to herself:

'The worthy Abbot of Aberbrothock
Had placed that bell on the Inchcape rock.
On a buoy in the storm it floated and swung,
And over the waves its warning rung.'

The occupation grew so monotonous that she began to feel as if she had been on the cliff for weeks. After what seemed an absolute slice out of eternity, there came a "Hello!" on the path behind her. She stopped ringing and jumped to her feet.

"Bevis! It's never you!"

"Mavis! Did you do all this for me? You trump!"

"Did you hear my bell, then, on the sea?"

"Of course I did, and it gave me my right reckoning. I hardly knew where I was. I might have been on the rocks without. Mrs. Penruddock told me about it, and I came at once to fetch you back."

"I wonder you didn't go to tell Romola you were safe!"

"Romola! Why on earth should I tell Romola?"

Mavis did not reply all at once.

"Only because I thought you seemed particularly interested in her!" she said at last.

Bevis looked frankly puzzled, then his face cleared and he drew a small photo from his pocket.

"Did Clive send you one of these?"

"He did!"

"Well, don't you know who the girl is? Can't you see it's Clive? Clive, dressed up in Romola's togs! Those are hardly Romola's boots, are they? We nearly died with laughing over it. He looked too killing for words. It was Madox who took the snap with Clive's camera."

Mavis, examining the photo by the light of these explanations, had little difficulty in recognising her boy cousin. Bevis was roaring with laughter at the joke, then he suddenly grew serious.

"Mavis!" he said in dead earnest. "You never thought I'd go making such a silly ass of myself with little Romola? That's not in my line at all!"

It was Mavis who did the blushing.

"Look here! We may as well have this out between us. If there's ever to be a mistress at The Warren - and I hope there will some day - I know whom I'd choose! Why, it's Mavis, the one who was good to me when I'd hardly a friend in the world or a name to call myself by, who didn't despise me for being a nobody, and wasn't ashamed to walk with me through the village, and who's kept me off more rocks than she's any idea of, besides what she's done for me to-day! If I asked her some day to think it over, do you fancy she might answer 'yes'?"

Choose from Thousands of 1stWorldLibrary Classics By

A. M. Barnard	C. M. Ingleby	Elizabeth Gaskell
Ada Leverson	Carolyn Wells	Elizabeth McCracken
Adolphus William Ward	Catherine Parr Traill	Elizabeth Von Arnim
Aesop	Charles A. Eastman	Ellem Key
Agatha Christie	Charles Amory Beach	Emerson Hough
Alexander Aaronsohn	Charles Dickens	Emilie F. Carlen
Alexander Kielland	Charles Dudley Warner	Emily Dickinson
Alexandre Dumas	Charles Farrar Browne	Enid Bagnold
Alfred Gatty	Charles Ives	Enilor Macartney Lane
Alfred Ollivant	Charles Kingsley	Erasmus W. Jones
Alice Duer Miller	Charles Klein	Ernie Howard Pie
Alice Turner Curtis	Charles Hanson Towne	Ethel May Dell
Alice Dunbar	Charles Lathrop Pack	Ethel Turner
Allen Chapman	Charles Romyn Dake	Ethel Watts Mumford
Ambrose Bierce	Charles Whibley	Eugenie Foa
Amelia E. Barr	Charles Willing Beale	Eugene Wood
Amory H. Bradford	Charlotte M. Braeme	Eustace Hale Ball
Andrew Lang	Charlotte M. Yonge	Evelyn Everett-green
Andrew McFarland Davis	Charlotte Perkins Stetson	Everard Cotes
Andy Adams	Clair W. Hayes	F. H. Cheley
Anna Alice Chapin	Clarence Day Jr.	F. J. Cross
Anna Sewell	Clarence E. Mulford	F. Marion Crawford
Annie Besant	Clemence Housman	Federick Austin Ogg
Annie Hamilton Donnell	Confucius	Ferdinand Ossendowski
Annie Payson Call	Coningsby Dawson	Francis Bacon
Annie Roe Carr	Cornelis DeWitt Wilcox	Francis Darwin
Annonaymous	Cyril Burleigh	Frances Hodgson Burnett
Anton Chekhov	D. H. Lawrence	Frances Parkinson Keyes
Arnold Bennett	Daniel Defoe	Frank Gee Patchin
Arthur Conan Doyle	David Garnett	Frank Harris
Arthur M. Winfield	Dinah Craik	Frank Jewett Mather
Arthur Ransome	Don Carlos Janes	Frank L. Packard
Arthur Schnitzler	Donald Keyhoe	Frank V. Webster
Atticus	Dorothy Kilner	Frederic Stewart Isham
B.H. Baden-Powell	Dougan Clark	Frederick Trevor Hill
B. M. Bower	Douglas Fairbanks	Frederick Winslow Taylor
B. C. Chatterjee	E. Nesbit	Friedrich Kerst
Baroness Emmuska Orczy	E.P.Roe	Friedrich Nietzsche
Baroness Orczy	E. Phillips Oppenheim	Fyodor Dostoyevsky
Basil King	Earl Barnes	G.A. Henty
Bayard Taylor	Edgar Rice Burroughs	G.K. Chesterton
Ben Macomber	Edith Van Dyne	Gabrielle E. Jackson
Bertha Muzzy Bower	Edith Wharton	Garrett P. Serviss
Bjornstjerne Bjornson	Edward Everett Hale	Gaston Leroux
Booth Tarkington	Edward J. O'Biren	George A. Warren
Boyd Cable	Edward S. Ellis	George Ade
Bram Stoker	Edwin L. Arnold	Geroge Bernard Shaw
C. Collodi	Eleanor Atkins	George Durston
C. E. Orr	Eliot Gregory	George Ebers

George Eliot
George Gissing
George MacDonald
George Meredith
George Orwell
George Sylvester Viereck
George Tucker
George W. Cable
George Wharton James
Gertrude Atherton
Gordon Casserly
Grace E. King
Grace Gallatin
Grace Greenwood
Grant Allen
Guillermo A. Sherwell
Gulielma Zollinger
Gustav Flaubert
H. A. Cody
H. B. Irving
H.C. Bailey
H. G. Wells
H. H. Munro
H. Irving Hancock
H. Rider Haggard
H. W. C. Davis
Haldeman Julius
Hall Caine
Hamilton Wright Mabie
Hans Christian Andersen
Harold Avery
Harold McGrath
Harriet Beecher Stowe
Harry Castlemon
Harry Coghill
Harry Houidini
Hayden Carruth
Helent Hunt Jackson
Helen Nicolay
Hendrik Conscience
Hendy David Thoreau
Henri Barbusse
Henrik Ibsen
Henry Adams
Henry Ford
Henry Frost
Henry James
Henry Jones Ford
Henry Seton Merriman
Henry W Longfellow
Herbert A. Giles

Herbert Carter
Herbert N. Casson
Herman Hesse
Hildegard G. Frey
Homer
Honore De Balzac
Horace B. Day
Horace Walpole
Horatio Alger Jr.
Howard Pyle
Howard R. Garis
Hugh Lofting
Hugh Walpole
Humphry Ward
Ian Maclaren
Inez Haynes Gillmore
Irving Bacheller
Isabel Hornibrook
Israel Abrahams
Ivan Turgenev
J.G.Austin
J. Henri Fabre
J. M. Barrie
J. Macdonald Oxley
J. S. Fletcher
J. S. Knowles
J. Storer Clouston
Jack London
Jacob Abbott
James Allen
James Andrews
James Baldwin
James Branch Cabell
James DeMille
James Joyce
James Lane Allen
James Lane Allen
James Oliver Curwood
James Oppenheim
James Otis
James R. Driscoll
Jane Austen
Jane L. Stewart
Janet Aldridge
Jens Peter Jacobsen
Jerome K. Jerome
John Burroughs
John Cournos
John F. Kennedy
John Gay
John Glasworthy

John Habberton
John Joy Bell
John Kendrick Bangs
John Milton
John Philip Sousa
Jonas Lauritz Idemil Lie
Jonathan Swift
Joseph A. Altsheler
Joseph Carey
Joseph Conrad
Joseph E. Badger Jr
Joseph Hergesheimer
Joseph Jacobs
Jules Vernes
Julian Hawthrone
Julie A Lippmann
Justin Huntly McCarthy
Kakuzo Okakura
Kenneth Grahame
Kenneth McGaffey
Kate Langley Bosher
Kate Langley Bosher
Katherine Cecil Thurston
Katherine Stokes
L. A. Abbot
L. T. Meade
L. Frank Baum
Latta Griswold
Laura Dent Crane
Laura Lee Hope
Laurence Housman
Lawrence Beasley
Leo Tolstoy
Leonid Andreyev
Lewis Carroll
Lewis Sperry Chafer
Lilian Bell
Lloyd Osbourne
Louis Hughes
Louis Tracy
Louisa May Alcott
Lucy Fitch Perkins
Lucy Maud Montgomery
Luther Benson
Lydia Miller Middleton
Lyndon Orr
M. Corvus
M. H. Adams
Margaret E. Sangster
Margret Howth
Margaret Vandercook

Margret Penrose
Maria Edgeworth
Maria Thompson Daviess
Mariano Azuela
Marion Polk Angellotti
Mark Overton
Mark Twain
Mary Austin
Mary Catherine Crowley
Mary Cole
Mary Hastings Bradley
Mary Roberts Rinehart
Mary Rowlandson
M. Wollstonecraft Shelley
Maud Lindsay
Max Beerbohm
Myra Kelly
Nathaniel Hawthrone
Nicolo Machiavelli
O. F. Walton
Oscar Wilde
Owen Johnson
P.G. Wodehouse
Paul and Mabel Thorne
Paul G. Tomlinson
Paul Severing
Percy Brebner
Peter B. Kyne
Plato
R. Derby Holmes
R. L. Stevenson
R. S. Ball
Rabindranath Tagore
Rahul Alvares
Ralph Bonehill
Ralph Henry Barbour
Ralph Victor
Ralph Waldo Emmerson
Rene Descartes
Rex Beach

Rex E. Beach
Richard Harding Davis
Richard Jefferies
Richard Le Gallienne
Robert Barr
Robert Frost
Robert Gordon Anderson
Robert L. Drake
Robert Lansing
Robert Lynd
Robert Michael Ballantyne
Robert W. Chambers
Rosa Nouchette Carey
Rudyard Kipling
Samuel B. Allison
Samuel Hopkins Adams
Sarah Bernhardt
Sarah C. Hallowell
Selma Lagerlof
Sherwood Anderson
Sigmund Freud
Standish O'Grady
Stanley Weyman
Stella Benson
Stella M. Francis
Stephen Crane
Stewart Edward White
Stijn Streuvels
Swami Abhedananda
Swami Parmananda
T. S. Ackland
T. S. Arthur
The Princess Der Ling
Thomas A. Janvier
Thomas A Kempis
Thomas Anderton
Thomas Bailey Aldrich
Thomas Bulfinch
Thomas De Quincey
Thomas Dixon

Thomas H. Huxley
Thomas Hardy
Thomas More
Thornton W. Burgess
U. S. Grant
Valentine Williams
Various Authors
Vaughan Kester
Victor Appleton
Victoria Cross
Virginia Woolf
Wadsworth Camp
Walter Camp
Walter Scott
Washington Irving
Wilbur Lawton
Wilkie Collins
Willa Cather
Willard F. Baker
William Dean Howells
William le Queux
W. Makepeace Thackeray
William W. Walter
William Shakespeare
Winston Churchill
Yei Theodora Ozaki
Yogi Ramacharaka
Young E. Allison
Zane Grey